May–Aug 2025

Day by Day with God

Rooting women's lives in the Bible

BRF Ministries

15 The Chambers, Vineyard
Abingdon OX14 3FE
+44 (0)1865 319700 | brf.org.uk

Bible Reading Fellowship is a charity (233280)
and company limited by guarantee (301324),
registered in England and Wales

EU Authorised Representative: Easy Access System Europe –
Mustamäe tee 50, 10621 Tallinn, Estonia, **gpsr.requests@easproject.com**

ISBN 978 1 80039 363 9
All rights reserved

This edition © 2025 Bible Reading Fellowship
Cover photo © istockphoto.com/SolStock

Distributed in Australia by:
MediaCom Education Inc, PO Box 610, Unley, SA 5061
Tel: 1 800 811 311 | admin@mediacom.org.au

Distributed in New Zealand by:
Scripture Union Wholesale, PO Box 760, Wellington
Tel: 04 385 0421 | suwholesale@clear.net.nz

Acknowledgements
Scripture quotations marked with the following abbreviations are taken from the version shown. Where no abbreviation is given, the quotation is taken from the same version as the headline reference. NIV: The Holy Bible, New International Version (Anglicised edition) copyright © 1979, 1984, 2011 by Biblica. Used by permission of Hodder & Stoughton Publishers, a Hachette UK company. All rights reserved. 'NIV' is a registered trademark of Biblica. UK trademark number 1448790. NLT: The Holy Bible, New Living Translation, copyright © 1996, 2004, 2007, 2013. Used by permission of Tyndale House Publishers, Inc., Carol Stream, Illinois 60188. All rights reserved. NRSV: The New Revised Standard Version Updated Edition. Copyright © 2021 National Council of Churches of Christ in the United States of America. Used by permission. All rights reserved worldwide. RSV: The Revised Standard Version of the Bible, copyright © 1946, 1952, 1971 by the Division of Christian Education of the National Council of the Churches of Christ in the United States of America. Used by permission. All rights reserved. AMP: The Amplified® Bible, Copyright © 2015 by The Lockman Foundation. Used by permission. www.Lockman.org. NKJV: the New King James Version®. Copyright © 1982 by Thomas Nelson. Used by permission. All rights reserved. ESV: The Holy Bible, English Standard Version, published by HarperCollins Publishers, © 2001 Crossway Bibles, a division of Good News Publishers. Used by permission. All rights reserved. MSG: *The Message*, copyright © 1993, 1994, 1995, 1996, 2000, 2001, 2002 by Eugene H. Peterson. Used by permission of NavPress. All rights reserved. Represented by Tyndale House Publishers, Inc. TLB: The Living Bible copyright © 1971 by Tyndale House Foundation. Used by permission of Tyndale House Publishers Inc., Carol Stream, Illinois 60188. All rights reserved.

A catalogue record for this book is available from the British Library

Printed and bound by Zenith Media NP4 0DQ

Day by Day with God

Edited by **Jackie Harris** May–August 2025

6	**The ten commandments** Lakshmi Jeffreys	*1–10 May*
17	**Jesus said: 'I am ...'** Jenny Sanders	*11–24 May*
32	**Amos: from shepherd to prophet** Amy Boucher Pye	*25–31 May*
40	**Mountains and valleys** Jen Baker	*1–14 June*
55	**What the Bible says about being a man** Chine McDonald	*15–28 June*
70	**Learning from the life of Ruth** Rosemary Green	*29 June–5 July*
78	**Making all things new: God's justice** Hannah Fytche	*6–19 July*
93	**How to make good decisions** Lyndall Bywater	*20 July–2 August*
108	**Amos: prophet for a disappointed God** Amy Boucher Pye	*3–9 August*
116	**Confidence in God** Catherine Butcher	*10–23 August*
131	**Paul's letter to the Philippians** Sara Batts-Neale	*24–31 August*

Writers in this issue

Lakshmi Jeffreys combines a number of roles within the home, church and wider community, including wife, mother, sister, vicar, friend and dog-walker. Her booklet on singleness was published shortly after she met the man she eventually married.

Jenny Sanders is an international speaker, prophetic teacher and writer. She has been discipling and training Jesus-lovers across streams and denominations for more than 30 years. She loves helping people grasp the magnificence of God's grace and the excitement of living life with him at the helm.

Amy Boucher Pye is a London-based writer, speaker, retreat leader and spiritual director. She's the author of several books and has an MA in Christian spirituality from the University of London. Find her at **amyboucherpye.com**.

Jen Baker is a speaker, author and mentor. Her mission is to see a global movement of Christian women living with courageous faith and creating kingdom impact.

Chine McDonald is a writer, a broadcaster and the director of the religious think tank Theos. A regular contributor to BBC Religion & Ethics programmes, she is also vice-chair of Greenbelt Festival and a trustee of Christian Aid.

Rosemary Green lives in Abingdon, where her ministry as a layperson is mainly among the elderly. A grandmother and great grandmother, she has been writing for BRF for 30 years, first for *New Daylight* and then for *Day by Day with God*.

Hannah Fytche is studying for her PhD in theology at the University of Cambridge. She has been writing for BRF Ministries since 2015, when she wrote her first book, *God's Daughters*, and has written for *Day by Day with God* since 2018.

Lyndall Bywater lives in Canterbury and works with The Salvation Army and the diocese of Canterbury, helping people pray. She is the author of two books, both published by BRF Ministries: *Faith in the Making* and *Prayer in the Making*.

Catherine Butcher is a writer and editor, an Anglican reader and a member of General Synod. The many books and magazines she has written focus on resourcing individuals and churches to make Jesus known.

Sara Batts-Neale is a priest in the diocese of Chelmsford. She is currently the Anglican chaplain to the University of Essex. Married to Tim, they live with a dog and host a cat.

Welcome

Having had a lot of decisions to make recently – and feeling this is not one of my strong points – I was particularly interested to read Lyndall Bywater's study on 'How to make decisions'. I found a lot of what she said really helpful and it made me think more broadly about how I read the Bible.

I confess there are times when it feels like a chore, when I sit with a passage and think, 'This isn't doing anything for me!' That's quite wrong, of course. First, it's more likely that it's touching a nerve, perhaps drawing me to think about something I don't want to consider. Second, it's changing me whether I am aware of it or not. Day by day, bit by bit, if I open my Bible with an open heart and mind, rather than an agenda, God's word will inform my attitudes and behaviour and teach me how to live according to God's ways. I find that really encouraging, and I'm learning that when reading the Bible feels hard, it's time to dig a little deeper.

I also find it helpful to have someone else's insights, which is where Bible reading notes like these come into their own. I can learn from others who have done their own reading and reflecting and are sharing what they have learned and how God has worked in their lives or the lives of people they know.

I'm very blessed to work with a wonderful team of writers who put a lot of care and prayer into the studies they write. We represent a diverse group of women from different backgrounds and with different ages and experiences, but we're united in our love for the scriptures and desire to learn from them and know them better.

As Lyndall reminds us in her Bible study, we probably won't find a verse that directly answers our dilemma or reflects our particular situation, but what we will find are verses that help us to see more clearly the God who loves us and wants to come alongside us whatever we are facing.

May these notes inspire you in your Bible reading, enable you to see God more clearly and draw you into his company.

Jackie

Jackie Harris, Editor

The ten commandments

Lakshmi Jeffreys writes…

The 1960s spy series *The Man from U.N.C.L.E* included a two-part special in which the villain wanted to conquer the world in the manner of Alexander the Great. His intention was to break each of the ten commandments as he did so. Most of us today would laugh at the ridiculous technology and gadgets. What might seem remarkable, however, is that someone who was not religious would be aware of the ten commandments.

When I ask some older people their thoughts or feelings about God, the response is sometimes, 'I don't believe in God, but I live by the ten commandments.' This statement implies that the commandments comprise a moral code. It also betrays a lack of knowledge, since the first four commandments relate directly to the God in whom the speaker does not believe! It's important to know that the ten commandments are not merely laws but describe the best relationship between God and God's people.

At our wedding, my husband and I promised to love, comfort, honour and protect each other. Our vows made our marriage legal, establishing the boundaries of our relationship within wider society, but our marriage is far richer than a set of rules to be obeyed. We are learning how to live together.

While marriage is a contract between equals, the covenant between God and God's people was not. Through Moses, God rescued the people enslaved in Egypt and brought them into the desert, on the way to the promised land, to learn how to be the people of God. God gave Moses two tablets of stone, on which the ten commandments were written.

The commandments are listed twice in the Bible (Exodus 20 and Deuteronomy 5), in the same order but with slightly different emphases. Just as vows state the parameters of a marriage, so the ten commandments gave the boundaries within which God's people could live in freedom in the land God had promised Abraham.

Sometimes Anglican churches use the commandments, each followed by words from the New Testament, as an introduction to confession. I have based the following studies on those New Testament verses. May we discover in the commandments God's loving acceptance and gentle challenge to be transformed by the Holy Spirit to live as disciples of Jesus.

THURSDAY 1 MAY MARK 12:28–33

I am the Lord your God

'God is one and there is no other but him. To love him with all your heart, with all your understanding and with all your strength, and to love your neighbour as yourself is more important than all burnt offerings and sacrifices.' (vv. 32–33, NIV)

The God who delivered the people from slavery in Egypt was not like other deities. This God was powerful and personal, a God of action and compassion. God had rescued them because God loved them. The relationship between God and God's people would be demonstrated in the love the people showed God and one another because God had set them free and was taking them to the promised land.

By Jesus' day, the law told people how to show love for God. There were rules about eating, drinking, washing, dressing and relating within and beyond the family. Every conceivable facet of life was governed by 'you must' or 'you must not'. In making the statement quoted, one insightful religious teacher realised that what mattered was not our behaviour towards God (religious rituals) but rather our awareness of who God is. God's people were called to faithful relationship, not following rules. As the religious teacher recognised something of who Jesus was, Jesus acknowledged the teacher was not far from the kingdom.

The kingdom of God is life with God in charge. Jesus brought the kingdom into being. To show we live in God's love, with God in charge, we are to love God, those around us and ourselves. In western society today, individual choice reigns supreme and the idea of God being in charge is uncomfortable. But if God is not in charge, then who is? All our choices are offered by someone or something, not always as obvious and certainly not as kind as the God who saves. Many of us make choices influenced by social media; medical, religious and social experts; governments and others. Perhaps as we become more familiar with God and the signs of God's kingdom, we will grow increasingly aware of how to choose with wisdom and love.

We spend time with or on what matters most to us. Ask God to save you from whatever takes your attention when you procrastinate instead of praying.

LAKSHMI JEFFREYS

FRIDAY 2 MAY   JOHN 4:1–26

Let nothing take God's place

'True worshippers will worship the Father in the Spirit and in truth, for they are the kind of worshippers the Father seeks. God is spirit, and his worshippers must worship in the Spirit and in truth.' (vv. 23–24, NIV)

French philosopher Voltaire said: 'In the beginning God created man in his own image, and man has been trying to repay the favour ever since.'

Having remembered who God is and what God had done, the people were told to express their love for God by worshipping only God. Fashioned in God's image, they knew him through his creating and saving actions, not by his appearance. Idols would limit God to a form God had created in the first place. Imagine a child preferring to spend time with a picture she had drawn of her mother, rather than spending time with her mum!

In Jesus' time, it was frowned upon for religious teachers (always male) to converse in public with women. Worse, Samaritans and Jews were sworn enemies. When Jesus asked this woman for a drink, he contravened all sorts of social and religious rules. Jesus challenged the woman's ideas about worship, allowing her to be honest about who she was as they spoke. To worship in spirit means to worship with everything: heart, mind, body and spirit. To worship in truth is to be honest before God. Jesus taught the woman to worship God as God is – not an image or an idea – and to come before God without any pretence.

We might not have a picture or model in front of us as we pray or sing to God, yet all of us have idols – something we put first in life. Family or friends, home, safety, health, work, leisure or even church are wonderful gifts from God, to be enjoyed fully but not put in the place of honest relationship with God. It is worth considering what or who comes first in your life and, if necessary, to confess this to God.

'And we all, who with unveiled faces contemplate the Lord's glory, are being transformed into his image' (2 Corinthians 3:18). Where is your gaze directed towards?

LAKSHMI JEFFREYS

SATURDAY 3 MAY   **HEBREWS 12:18–29**

Do not misuse God's name

Since we are receiving a kingdom that cannot be shaken, let us be thankful, and so worship God acceptably with reverence and awe, for our 'God is a consuming fire.' (vv. 28–29, NIV)

Anyone with a pet knows how stressful choosing a name can be. (It can be even worse when naming children!) Before our dog came to live with us, someone suggested calling her Kili, after a dwarf from *The Hobbit*. Since we all loved the book, and this was the most female-sounding name, the rest of us agreed. As soon as she was in our home, however, we noticed the puppy's striking physical characteristics. We were unanimous in deciding her actual name, which describes her perfectly.

Every culture has used names to depict character or lineage. In the ancient Near East, when the commandments were given, a name not only signified appearance or personality but also potency; to call on someone's name, especially the name of a deity, was to invoke their power. We have a similar approach today when the leader of an organisation might say to someone, 'Tell them I sent you.' The leader's name is sufficient to enable the other person to obtain access. The name has power. To use the name of the leader for purely personal gain would betray a relationship of trust.

In our passage, the writer reminds the Hebrew Christians that God was so holy that their ancestors were not allowed to touch the mountain on which God met Moses. God's Son Jesus, by his death on the cross, delivered people from sin, abolishing the need for rules and regulations. If the Hebrew Christians returned to following the law, they were ignoring what Jesus had done, losing sight of God and taking for granted their relationship with God. As characters in 'The Chronicles of Narnia' stories by C.S. Lewis constantly realised, 'Aslan is not a tame lion!' Relationship with God is not for our benefit but for God's glory.

When we pray in the name of Jesus, we are not using a magic formula. Instead, we are asking in line with who Jesus is. How does that alter your prayers?

LAKSHMI JEFFREYS

SUNDAY 4 MAY   **COLOSSIANS 3:1–17**

Holy sabbath

Since you have been raised to new life with Christ, set your sights on the realities of heaven, where Christ sits in the place of honour at God's right hand. Think about the things of heaven, not the things of earth. For you died to this life, and your real life is hidden with Christ in God. (vv.1–3, NLT)

The fourth commandment is to keep the sabbath day holy, working for six days and then enabling rest on the seventh. It is possibly the most ignored and least understood of the ten. Some people might have a day off to catch up with chores or undertake other duties, but there is little rest. Many women, especially if they are not in paid employment, believe they do not deserve a day off (no one says 'sabbath'), while women with commitments to caring or other duties might crave a weekly sabbath, but it seems impossible. Is this commandment obsolete in the 21st century?

Exodus and Deuteronomy differ in the reason for sabbath. Exodus instructs people to *remember* sabbath rest: God created the world in six days and God rested on the sabbath. People were created by God and thus are completely dependent on God. Given dominion over creation, people also enjoy the privilege of sharing God's rest. God rested – so should we.

Meanwhile, Deuteronomy commands the people to *observe* sabbath: God rescued the people from Egypt. They were enslaved so had no rest. Now people should keep sabbath rest to remember with thanksgiving God's deliverance. Sabbath reminds us who God is (creator) and what God has done (delivered his people from slavery).

The key to all the commandments is to focus on who God is and what God has done. Paul's words to the Colossian Christians are a reminder of how to relate to other people – with kindness, compassion, etc. We are called to love others as we love ourselves, enabled by God's love in Jesus and empowered by the Holy Spirit. To keep sabbath involves trusting God. For further insight, read *The Ruthless Elimination of Hurry* by John Mark Comer (Hodder and Stoughton, 2019).

God of love, forgive me for forgetting who you are and what you have done. Remind me to trust you daily with every person and situation in my life. Teach me to live from sabbath rest. Amen.

LAKSHMI JEFFREYS

MONDAY 5 MAY — **GALATIANS 6:1–10**

Honour your father and mother

So let's not get tired of doing what is good. At just the right time we will reap a harvest of blessing if we don't give up. Therefore, whenever we have the opportunity, we should do good to everyone – especially to those in the family of faith. (vv. 9–10, NLT)

This commandment is a positive instruction (something to do rather than a 'do not') and there will be beneficial consequences to the action. If you honour your mother and father, says God, you will live a long, full life in the land the Lord is giving God's people. The emphasis has moved from relationship with God to relating within the community God is growing. It is almost the practical outworking of the first commandment (see Thursday's notes). How I love my neighbour – including family – shows the reality and depth of my love for God.

In Moses' time, older people were respected because of their experience of life and God. Their role was to teach younger generations what it meant to honour God. With an emphasis on remembering what God had done, the commandments enabled the older people to share their memories of God's blessings, in order for the younger people to learn how to live God's way. In turn, the youngsters would be asked to share their wisdom and learning with future generations in the promised land.

It is difficult to translate the context of the commandments to 21st century western life. Old age is often feared, with the possibility of diminished physical and mental capacity. Conversely, youth and outward appearance and ability are revered. There is little room for learning from previous generations. Instead, each peer group must discover life on its own terms. Yet relationship thrives as we remember and learn from the past. Older Christians can teach children and children show respect to their forebears in faith. Doing good, as Paul encourages in our reading today, will happen as we live according to God's covenant – in relationship to God and thereby one another.

God of love, teach those of us who are older to share our experiences of who you are; teach those of us who are younger to listen to our 'faith parents', that all of us together might live in your kingdom. Amen.

LAKSHMI JEFFREYS

TUESDAY 6 MAY **ROMANS 13:1–10**

Do not murder

Love does no harm to a neighbour. Therefore love is the fulfilment of the law. (v. 10, NIV)

In most societies, the taking of human life is against the law. There are then exceptions for capital punishment, war and other situations when killing can be legally justified. Add heartbreaking cases of people on life-support machines or those who face euthanasia decisions and we are in a moral, legal and philosophical minefield. What is murder?

As the people were travelling through the wilderness, God was building a community based on God's covenant with them. They were learning how to live alongside one another, under God's rule and enjoying God's blessings. While there were regulations allowing execution, no individual could kill anyone else in the community for personal reasons. After all, each person was created in the image of God and life was a gift only God gave.

When Jesus taught about the commandments, he condemned both murder and speaking unkindly about anyone (Matthew 5:21–22). In his letter to the church in Rome, Paul explained how this might work in practice. Christians were to obey the law of the land as a minimum. They were also to love the people around them as God loved – not focusing on wrongdoing but seeing them as created in God's image and therefore worthy of love. It was while we were still sinners that Christ died for us, and no one is beyond redemption.

It is so very difficult to remember that the person who has committed a dreadful act was once a vulnerable baby, knit together by God in their mother's womb. Yet as we choose to see other people as those who have the image of God, however hidden, we will not murder them in our thoughts, feelings or words (where actions are formed). Instead, we shall learn to love as God loves.

Loving Jesus, you died for the 'godly' and the 'ungodly'. Teach me to see my sisters and brothers as you see them. May I entrust you with judgement, so that I might be free to love as you direct. Amen.

LAKSHMI JEFFREYS

WEDNESDAY 7 MAY 1 CORINTHIANS 6:12–20

Do not commit adultery

Do you not know that your bodies are temples of the Holy Spirit, who is in you, whom you have received from God? (v. 19, NIV)

Details have been changed in the following story. Cathy's desire to live an authentic Christian life led her to question the morality of accepting a car park ticket offered to her, in case she defrauded the council. In other areas of her life, however, things were not so clear. Cathy's husband struggled with their disabled child. He was angry in his new job and bitter that he was not a prominent church leader. Years later, Cathy confessed to a friend that her husband's physical, sexual and other abuse was bearable only because another man had noticed Cathy's unhappiness. Their subsequent adulterous relationship was both anathema to and a solace for Cathy.

Adultery is unfaithfulness in a committed relationship. Bible commentators suggest it is the social equivalent of the religious crime of having other gods. In our reading, Paul rightly condemns the sexual promiscuity of the church. The Corinthians (and we) have been bought at a price – Christ's death on the cross. What we do with our bodies matters because love for God, neighbour and self is demonstrated in physical actions. If the commandments are parameters within which Christians operate to show God's love, no single commandment can be highlighted above another. Sadly, we often 'tut' about adultery in ways we do not about murder or keeping sabbath.

Adultery should not be justified, whatever the circumstances. At the same time, God is judge, not us. As I pray for Cathy and her family, I imagine Jesus telling her that he does not condemn her, as he told the woman about to be stoned in John 8. And as I pray, I cry out to God for my sisters in abusive relationships and for God's people to offer sanctuary, healing and hope.

God of judgement and hope, I confess my tendency to condemn people who are unfaithful in relationship. Teach me compassion and please bring freedom to my sisters in abusive relationships. Amen.

LAKSHMI JEFFREYS

THURSDAY 8 MAY 1 TIMOTHY 6:6–21

Do not steal

They are to do good, to be rich in good works, generous, and ready to share, thus storing up for themselves the treasure of a good foundation for the future, so that they may take hold of the life that really is life. (vv. 18–19, NRSV)

In my research, I discovered the commandment not to steal concerned relationship, rather than property. If someone was kidnapped, they were removed from God's community and thereby relationship with God – a clear violation of the covenant. God delivered his people into freedom. To kidnap or otherwise take another person was to violate God's actions.

Tragically, every day there are stories from around the world of kidnapping, hijacking and other ways in which people are stolen. Certainly, a ransom demand involves indirectly stealing money, property or sometimes power, for example, when young girls are taken from their schools by religious extremists. But stealing people can be more subtle than kidnap or hijack. Perhaps stealing is to manipulate someone else for personal gain. Zero hours contracts or crazy demands by employers to ensure employees are always on call steal people from their families and friends, all for monetary gain. Modern day slavery plumbs further depths.

Once again, we are called to focus on God, not on 'stuff'. We are back in 'idol' territory and the outworking of the second commandment. Paul reminds Timothy that 'the love of money is a root of all kinds of evil' (v. 10). Timothy is charged to pursue Jesus and all godliness, and to avoid the temptation to idolise wealth or possessions. As we focus on God, we discover what true riches are – treasures in heaven, as Jesus called them. While stealing destroys relationships, pursuit of godliness builds community around the cross of Christ and offers life. Jesus came to bring us life in all its fullness (John 10:10), so we have no need to steal or manipulate as we look to him.

Pray for the work of International Justice Mission and other organisations seeking to bring people to freedom from slavery. Pray also for Christians working in employment law and related areas.

LAKSHMI JEFFREYS

FRIDAY 9 MAY   **EPHESIANS 4:17–32**

Do not tell lies about others

Therefore each of you must put off falsehood and speak truthfully to your neighbour, for we are all members of one body. (v. 25, NIV)

God's people were vulnerable as they travelled to the promised land. Their community was far smaller than those of surrounding peoples. It was essential that they were united and could trust one another. To lie about someone, as they travelled through hostile territory, was therefore tantamount to murder because either the speaker or the victim of the lies would have to be evicted and they would not survive alone.

There are similarities between God's people in the wilderness and the church in Ephesus. The Ephesian Christians had been saved by faith in Jesus from a pagan society. They lived amid people whose lifestyle they had once shared. Through Paul, God was teaching them about how to live as a community of believers. This transformation begins in the mind – the focus of our thoughts determines our actions (see Tuesday's notes). The way the church behaved towards one another would demonstrate their love in response to God's love for them. Just as the Israelites in the wilderness needed to be united and trusting of one another, so the Ephesians were to be truthful in all their dealings. Lying about a fellow believer would destroy the community, as well as the individual.

Sadly, even within our churches, people speak *about* others rather than *to* them. Years ago, I said something which deeply offended someone, who told a friend that they would never return to church while I was there. Later they explained to me that they did not tell the truth about the impact of what I had said in case they hurt my feelings. Had they told me how much I had hurt them, there might have been reconciliation. Instead, the result of this (in their words 'white') lie was sadness and fracture in the body of Christ.

Gracious God, forgive me for speaking about people, rather than addressing my words to them. Give me the courage to avoid gossip and lies and instead to speak and receive the truth in love. Amen.

LAKSHMI JEFFREYS

SATURDAY 10 MAY   **ACTS 20:17–36**

Do not be greedy for what others have

'And I have been a constant example of how you can help those in need by working hard. You should remember the words of the Lord Jesus: "It is more blessed to give than to receive."' (v. 35, NLT)

The advertising business is built on covetousness. We are sold not a car or shoes or a phone, but a lifestyle to be maintained. There is a craving in society to be seen to be significant, someone special, fuelling the lie that longing can be fulfilled through objects or particular relationships. Celebrity culture in politics, entertainment and elsewhere promotes image over substance. The internet and other media are used brutally to destroy that image, should the celebrity fall foul of expectations. At the heart of covetousness is desire – for a particular person, object or existence. Rather than living with thankfulness, we compare what we have and who we are to those around us and end up wanting more or better.

Notice the emphasis of Paul's words in our passage. He is not concerned about what he has but whom he serves. There are frequent references to being led by the Holy Spirit. Paul is crystal clear about his purpose and that does not allow any comparison with the people he has encountered. Although he knows he will suffer for the gospel, he is content to be a servant of Christ. In fact, he warns the Ephesian church that they too will encounter difficulties.

When we are secure in our relationship with God, thankful for what Jesus has done and trusting the Holy Spirit to guide us, we are free to focus on ways in which we can love our neighbours. We can choose to serve from a position of confidence in Christ rather than needing to fill an ache inside. As beloved daughters of the living God, we are free to explore and enjoy life in all its fullness.

Almighty God, you have made us for yourself, and our hearts are restless till they find their rest in you. Pour your love into our hearts and draw us to yourself, that we may be content. Amen. (After St Augustine)

LAKSHMI JEFFREYS

Jesus said: 'I am...'

Jenny Sanders writes…

Identity is a hot topic right now. People everywhere are searching for theirs.

In childhood we experiment with different personae, pretending to be all sorts of people, from train drivers and explorers to famous singers and sports personalities.

Much of this falls away during adolescence as we begin to work out where and how we fit, while forming our own ideas and opinions about the world. By the end of our teenage years we are usually significantly clearer about who we are as an individual – not just someone's offspring or sibling but a person in our own right with valid thoughts, feelings and ambitions.

Conversely, in adulthood we may try to hide who we are. Perhaps we feel insecure or are nervous about voicing our convictions for fear we might be ridiculed or shut down. However, when life inevitably throws us challenges, who we really are deep down rises to the surface and becomes evident.

Jesus was totally secure in who he was and what he did. John's gospel tells us that just before Jesus washed his disciples' feet, 'Jesus knew that the Father had put all things under his power, and that he had come from God and was returning to God' (John 13:3, NIV). That confidence in his identity allowed Jesus to take water and a towel and do the job of a servant: washing the dusty, sweaty feet of his disciples.

While Jesus rested in who he was, others were less sure. When he asked his followers who the crowds thought he was, the replies were mixed: 'Some say John the Baptist; others say Elijah; and still others, Jeremiah or one of the prophets' (Matthew 16:14, NIV). They recognised that there was something special about this man from Galilee, but they couldn't quite see the truth.

Of the twelve, it was Peter who had a divine revelation: 'You are the Messiah, the Son of the living God' (Matthew 16:16, NIV). He received a blessing from Jesus for such an assured faith statement.

Seven times in the gospel of John, Jesus reveals different facets of his nature and calling using pictures and metaphors. Over the next fortnight, we'll unpack those 'I am' statements, with the understanding that each one echoes the words of Exodus 3:14 where God tells Moses, 'I am who I am.' That use of the present tense points to God's eternal existence manifested through Jesus. He is as real today as ever.

SUNDAY 11 MAY   JOHN 6:5–13; 25–40

Bread for life

'I am the bread of life.' (v. 35, NIV)

Don't you love the smell of freshly baked bread? It's one of my favourite smells. I find a loaf of artisan bread a better gift than flowers or chocolates.

For the people on the hillside by the Sea of Galilee many years ago, it was a simple but welcome meal, accompanied by a few fish, after a day of listening to Jesus' teaching. Recognising that the crowd would be hungry, Jesus asked his followers where they could go to buy bread for everyone. The exorbitant cost of such an undertaking for 5,000 people (probably more if we include women and children), sent his disciples into a spin.

Fortunately, one generous little boy was prepared to give Jesus the food he had brought. Jesus took his offering of bread and fish and, after thanking God for this provision, miraculously multiplied it so no one went without. What a story that lad had to tell when he got home!

Everybody had their fill, and twelve baskets of leftovers were gathered up by the disciples. Nevertheless, by the next morning every single one of those people would have been hungry again and keen for breakfast. Every culture has their equivalent of this basic foodstuff, be it a chapati, a roti or a naan. It's the simplest of foods, but it can satisfy our hunger and keep us alive.

Physical nourishment is one thing, but we are created with a spiritual appetite too. When Jesus referred to himself as bread, he was offering something more satisfying and substantial than plain bread. Jesus encouraged the people to find their spiritual sustenance in him. He still does. Daily digging in with him, nurturing our connection with him, provides everything that we need to feed our souls, to live a life of faith and walk in open, clean relationship with him.

Heavenly Father, thank you that in you I can find everything I need to live the abundant life you've called me to. Please keep me hungry for more of you each day. Amen.

JENNY SANDERS

MONDAY 12 MAY   **EXODUS 16:13–31**

Bread in the wilderness

'It is not Moses who has given you the bread from heaven, but it is my Father who gives you the true bread from heaven. For the bread of God is the bread that comes down from heaven and gives life to the world.' (John 6:32–33, NIV)

A crucial part of Israel's history included God leading them out of 400 years of captivity in Egypt, from slavery to freedom, through the wilderness, into the land first promised to Abraham. Under the leadership of Moses, they spent 40 years in the Judean wilderness learning to rely on God for all their needs.

This included the miraculous provision of bread which they called 'manna', from the Hebrew '*Mann hou?*' meaning, 'What is this?' Exodus 16:31 describes it as 'white like coriander seed and [it] tasted like wafers made with honey'. There may not have been much variety on that wilderness menu but there was always just the right quantity for everyone. The people soon found a way to crush and cook the raw ingredient into a cake-like product which 'tasted like something made with olive oil' (Numbers 11:8). There was obviously enough nutritional value in it to sustain them through the long trek, but nevertheless, the people grumbled about it. I imagine it became rather a monotonous diet day after day.

Inevitably, they began to take their miraculous provision for granted. Sadly, I see myself in this story. Do you? Like the Israelites, I all too easily slip into taking God's provision for granted. I am ashamed to often find myself more prone to grumbling than to thankfulness.

The manna served as a symbol of Jesus, the bread of life. It had to be gathered daily, but there was always enough. I know that when I set time aside to meet with Jesus it brings me spiritual life, just as bread brings me physical nourishment. Any routine can become stale and meaningless, but a thankful heart is one that produces joy as it focuses on the one who provides for us each day.

When did you last feast on Jesus, the bread of life? Which things are prone to squeeze him out of your life? How might you change that? Take some time now to thank him for his goodness to you.

JENNY SANDERS

TUESDAY 13 MAY JOHN 8:12–19

The light of the world

'I am the light of the world. Whoever follows me will never walk in darkness, but will have the light of life.' (v. 12, NIV)

I've spent a lot of time in South Africa, where we experience daily power cuts, or 'load-shedding', which regularly plunge us into darkness for several hours at a time. In those periods, we are grateful for the beam of a torch, the light from a phone or even the flicker of a candle. The dimmest glow can relieve total darkness.

In Jesus' day, the country was under enemy occupation; the sense of menacing oppression and darkness was ever-present as Roman soldiers policed the streets. Justice was rough, tradition despised and taxes had to be paid to the subjugators.

When Jesus began his ministry, the religious elite failed to recognise who he really was, but ordinary people began to wonder whether he might actually be the Messiah they longed for. A spark was ignited, a glimmer of hope at last. Jesus cut through the uncertainty when he boldly stated, 'I am the light of the world.' Despite the efforts of the Romans and Pharisees to crush him, John's words were true: 'The light shines in the darkness, and the darkness has not overcome it' (John 1:5).

Jesus shone meaning on ancient words, bringing life to the treasured scriptures of old. His stories illuminated things the Pharisees had over-complicated, which had often left people burdened by legalistic and dry rituals.

The light of Jesus brings us clarity. Having him in the driving seat of life allows us to see obstacles, anticipate hurdles and navigate life's challenges with confidence and faith. His light living inside us shines out as a guide to others too.

Around the globe many believers are ostracised, persecuted and imprisoned for their faith. Their world may feel very dark, but their frequent testimony is that nothing can extinguish the light and love of Jesus.

Consider the extraordinary power of light. You may feel small and ineffective, but remember that even the faintest glimmer of light can banish darkness. Pray that God's light would penetrate dark places today.

JENNY SANDERS

WEDNESDAY 14 MAY   **PSALM 119:105–112**

Lighting the way

Your word is a lamp for my feet, a light on my path. (v. 105, NIV)

I once lived in a small village that had no shops and no street lighting, just a church, a pub and a telephone box. I loved it; but during the winter we had to use our torches if we were to arrive home safely and injury-free. Perilous steps and a narrow pavement had to be navigated between the car park and the house. In the ice and snow it became even more treacherous.

I always liked to leave our porch light on. It shone out faithfully, acting as a guide. For me, it signified hope too – the warm familiarity of home; a safe place.

The path of life provides us with unforeseen obstacles and hidden challenges, but God's word provides us with the light we need to take the next step even through difficult terrain. The Bible serves as an effective torch, shedding light on our journey. It's packed full of timeless truths and unbreakable promises which hold fast regardless of the period of history in which we live.

We'd probably prefer a powerful spotlight to show us the whole journey ahead so that we can feel in control, but God chooses to provide us with just enough light for the next step as long as we stay in step with him. Walking closely and in intimacy with him, we are safe; we won't lose our footing. We'll resist the urge to either run ahead or to hang back in the darkness.

Jesus is the Word made flesh. He is the light that journeys with us, and his word shows us the way that will lead us safely to our heavenly home, avoiding metaphorical potholes, bogs and precipices along the way.

If you find yourself in a dark place today, reach for his word and reach for his hand to lead you on.

Thank God for the light of his word. Pray for the many people who work to translate the Bible so that others can enjoy God's light for themselves and have a copy in their own language.

JENNY SANDERS

THURSDAY 15 MAY JOHN 10:1–10

Gates and doors

'I am the gate for the sheep' (v. 7, NIV)

In first-century Palestine, shepherds and sheep were part of the landscape. Jews couldn't keep pigs, but sheep were a useful source of income. Their wool could be sold, spun and made into fabric; their meat could be eaten without contravening the law, and lambs were required for sin offerings and sacrifices.

At night, the sheep were brought into a walled sheepfold. The entrance and exit of this structure was narrow, allowing the passage of just one sheep at a time, so that every morning and evening the shepherd could check each one.

This is the allegory Jesus used when he was talking to the Pharisees. In the previous chapter, he had just restored the sight of a man born blind. The religious leaders, offended by both the man and his Sabbath healing, summoned his parents to corroborate the story. Although they admitted that this was their son, they wouldn't commit themselves any further, 'because they were afraid of the Jewish leaders, who already had decided that anyone who acknowledged that Jesus was the Messiah would be put out of the synagogue' (John 9:22).

The religious elite thought that they could decide who was either 'in' or 'out' of their circle. They set themselves up as the arbiters of who did or didn't deserve entry to God's house. In a sense they presented themselves as the door by which people could gain access to, and approval from, God. They were sorely mistaken.

Only Jesus is our doorway to God. We can't come to God any other way, because the forgiveness of our sins requires a sinless sacrifice. Not only has Jesus paid the ultimate price to make possible an authentic relationship with God, but he also remains in place as that unique doorway.

Think about how many times a day you use a door. While we only need to accept Jesus as Lord once, we can access God through Jesus and the Holy Spirit every day. What a privilege.

JENNY SANDERS

FRIDAY 16 MAY   **JOHN 10:1–10**

Point of entry

So Jesus again said to them, 'Truly, truly, I say to you, I am the door of the sheep.' (v. 7, RSV)

Visit a historic building, and you'll probably go in through an ornate door, maybe carved from ancient oak or sporting brass embellishments. You may have been greeted and perhaps your ticket was checked before you were handed a brochure. Without a ticket you would be denied entry.

Such doors are usually impressive. Stable doors and sheep pen doors, however, are rustic, rudimentary and functional.

In this passage, Jesus claims to be the doorway to God the Father; the one legitimate point of entry. Thieves and bandits might try to climb over the wall or gain access another way, but only the shepherd can grant authorised entry.

The threshold of any property is the place where we are met by the host(s). The door is where we are welcomed with warmth and delight. It's disappointing to visit friends unannounced and find that the door remains firmly closed because everyone is elsewhere. Another time when you come by the door may be flung wide, hugs given and received and, before you know it, you're in the heart of the home enjoying an enthusiastic welcome and winsome hospitality.

Jesus says that this is the kind of welcome which takes place when someone submits their life to him and joins the family. No one who comes to Jesus is left waiting on a cold doorstep; heaven throws a party as they are welcomed in through repentance and faith in Jesus' finished work on the cross. Jesus said, 'I tell you, there is rejoicing in the presence of the angels of God over one sinner who repents' (Luke 15:10, NIV). I imagine that's quite a party!

We don't need to hammer incessantly on this door; Jesus is just a whisper away, eager to welcome those who come truly seeking him.

Father God, thank you for accepting me into your family. Lord Jesus, I thank you that you are the door through which I can walk each day to both know God and be known by him. Amen.

JENNY SANDERS

SATURDAY 17 MAY JOHN 10:11–18

The good shepherd

'I am the good shepherd. The good shepherd lays down his life for the sheep.' (v. 11, NIV)

A first-century shepherd needed to be of a certain calibre. They didn't just sit around admiring the scenery while inspiring artists to capture whimsical pastoral scenes on canvas.

Shepherds were responsible for seeking out good pasture and sufficient fresh water for the flock. They would go ahead of them, leading them to safe grazing places while being continually on the alert for predators. Defending the vulnerable from fierce bears and opportunistic lions looking to snatch a sheep kept them on high alert. Not only must a shepherd protect his sheep, but they would also need to find the ones that went astray, rescue those that got stuck in a ditch, down a hole, had stumbled over a wall or slipped down an escarpment. They would walk miles, be used to roughing it outdoors and have the skills to nurse a sick sheep back to health, set a broken bone and help the ewes in lambing time.

By likening himself to a shepherd, Jesus wonderfully illustrates facets of his own character. A good shepherd, unlike a hired hand who would simply look out for his own interests, consistently puts the needs of their flock before their own and protects them at all costs. That means that his life is on the line each day and if it comes to it, he will die rather than let a single sheep be harmed.

Jesus is clearly that shepherd, while we are the sheep who are prone to wander. I know there are times when I don't feel close to God at all; times when I've made poor decisions, been selfish, ignored his voice and let him down. I'm so thankful that he's never given up on me. His grace has always searched me out and welcomed me back into the fold.

Thank you, Jesus, that you are the ultimate good shepherd. I am so grateful that you gave your life for me so that although I was lost, I am now found. May I never stray from your tender care. Amen.

JENNY SANDERS

SUNDAY 18 MAY JOHN 10:22–30

Tuning in and listening up

'My sheep listen to my voice; I know them, and they follow me.'
(v. 27, NIV)

Have you ever been in a crowded room and suddenly realised that, despite the hubbub of conversation, your spouse, your child or your friend is there too? You may not be able to see them, but you have picked out their voice in the melee.

When you know someone intimately, you automatically tune in to their voice, even when there are other voices operating at equal volume. You know the tone, pitch and intonation of your loved ones so well that you can quickly zone in on them.

Sheep do this too. While multiple flocks may have shared a sheep pen overnight, huddling together for warmth and protection, in the morning each shepherd would call to his own to lead them out into the new day and towards fresh pasture. They are so familiar with the voice of their own shepherd that they won't respond to another one. Relying on him as they do for sustenance and care, theirs is a relationship of total trust. They have heard his voice each day for all their lives; why would they follow the voice of someone else?

How well are we able to discern the voice of Jesus above all the other voices that clamour for our attention each day from social media, news feeds and advertisements? The best way to distinguish one voice from another is to spend more time with that individual. Frequency breeds familiarity, which is why the timbre of our family is the one we tend to pick up above all the rest.

Spending time in God's presence, reading and studying his word, soaking ourselves in his truths and understanding his character are all ways that help us tune in to what he is saying to us. His is the voice we need to hear.

When did you last hear Jesus' voice clearly? What did he say to you? How can you increase your ability to discern his voice above all others?

JENNY SANDERS

MONDAY 19 MAY   **JOHN 11:1, 4–6, 14–15, 20–44**

The last enemy defeated

'I am the resurrection and the life. The one who believes in me will live, even though they die; and whoever lives by believing in me will never die. Do you believe this?' (vv. 25–26, NIV)

I've always found this a curious passage. Hearing that his friend Lazarus was sick, Jesus said, 'This illness will not end in death' (v. 4) and stayed where he was. Then, on the way to Bethany, he told his disciples that Lazarus had actually died.

By the time Jesus arrived, Lazarus had been entombed for four days. The sisters were heartbroken; Mary couldn't even bring herself to come and meet him. The account oozes sorrowful disappointment. Martha, however (who is often presented as less spiritual thanks to the story in Luke 10:38–42), hurried out to express her unwavering confidence in Jesus, declaring: 'If you had been here, my brother would not have died… even now God will give you whatever you ask' (vv. 21–22). She had her theological ducks in a row, believing Lazarus would rise again 'at the last day' (v. 24).

Jesus cut through it all with his next words: 'I am the resurrection and the life' (v. 25). Although he had not yet been to the cross and broken out from his tomb in an earth-shattering resurrection, in Jesus lay the God-ordained power for victory over death. His statement hints at this.

The Bible calls death 'the last enemy' (1 Corinthians 15:26) – the thing that gets us all in the end – but in Jesus this is not the end. Raising Lazarus to life dynamically demonstrated this truth and God's glory, and it showed Jesus' love for Lazarus and his two sisters. No one could deny that a dead man was now alive again.

The crucifixion, resurrection and ascension of Jesus paved the way for our spiritual resurrection when we join God's family. It also gives us unwavering hope beyond our own inevitable death. We have the glorious certainty of eternal life in a perfect heaven shared with him.

Thank you, Lord Jesus, that in you lies the power to conquer death itself. Thank you for the hope you have put in our hearts by bringing life from death. Amen.

JENNY SANDERS

TUESDAY 20 MAY   **LUKE 24:1–8; JOHN 20:1–18**

Resurrection morning

'He is not here; he has risen!' (Luke 24:6, NIV)

What a discovery the women made that first Easter Sunday! The empty tomb gave them cause for alarm, then grief, then fear, followed by awe and wonder. They moved from anxiety about the location of his body to concern that it had been taken away, and then to an encounter with the gardener who turned out to be the risen Saviour.

I love the way that Mary recognised Jesus when he said her name, whereas the two disciples on the way to Emmaus had the best Bible study in history and still failed to realise who was delivering it (Luke 24:13–32). How amazing that God calls us by name too.

Scholars have spent years studying the reality of the resurrection. No other explanation holds up. The apostle Paul wrote in depth to the church at Corinth on the topic. If it didn't happen, he says, then 'your faith is futile; you are still in your sins' (1 Corinthians 15:17). By dying and rising again, Jesus conquered the power of sin, death and hell, giving us certain hope – something 'divinely guaranteed' (Hebrews 11:1, AMP) – for life beyond this one. Jesus told us he has gone to prepare a place for us so that we can spend eternity in his company (John 14:3). What could be better?

The well-known verse John 3:16 tells us why Jesus died: 'For God so loved the world that he gave his one and only Son, that whoever believes in him shall not perish but have eternal life.' Paul tells Timothy that Christ 'has destroyed death' (2 Timothy 1:10); it's been abolished forever for those who have accepted the salvation gift.

Heaven is not wishful thinking – a happy thought to soothe the grieving – but a perfect reality we can enjoy forever. Paradise, indeed.

Heaven is not about floating aimlessly on clouds. It's eternal intimacy with the King of kings – a place of perfection without tears, pain or death. Read Revelation 21:3–4 and thank God for the certainty we carry.

JENNY SANDERS

WEDNESDAY 21 MAY — JOHN 13:34—14:7

Abundant life

Jesus answered, 'I am the way and the truth and the life. No one comes to the Father except through me.' (v. 6, NIV)

After Jesus predicted his death and Peter's denial, his disciples were confused. Jesus comforted them with these familiar words.

His followers found talk of Jesus' departure deeply disturbing. They wanted to be with him wherever he planned to travel next; they didn't understand that he had a divine appointment at the cross, where he would pay for the sins of the world once and for all.

Peter was so passionate about his desire to stay close to his master that he overstated his position: 'I will lay down my life for you' (John 13:37), he claimed. We know only too well how that turned out. Peter denied he even knew Jesus, not once, but three times.

We've all had questions about life. The world is consumed with looking for answers, though often in the wrong places. We all yearn for a secure, safe path through life; we long to hear words of truth and integrity rather than obfuscation and lies from those in national and international leadership, and from those closer to home. All of us carry the conviction somewhere deep inside ourselves that we were made for more than an arid existence.

Jesus embodies all of the solutions to our searching. He is the one through whom we can have a living relationship with God. Following his personally designed paths keeps us safe. He speaks with tender compassion, but always with unchanging truth. Ephesians 2:10 says: 'We are God's handiwork, created in Christ Jesus to do good works, which God prepared in advance for us to do.' God is not desperately searching for a job he can give us, but longs for us to discover who he has made us to be so we can flourish and live 'more abundantly' (John 10:10, NKJV). Who wouldn't want that?

What would you say to someone who is searching for a way to navigate their life well? How might Jesus' words encourage them, and you, today?

JENNY SANDERS

THURSDAY 22 MAY   **JOHN 14:1–14**

The meaning of life

Jesus answered, 'I am the way and the truth and the life. No one comes to the Father except through me.' (v. 6, NIV)

It's a bold claim. Jesus said that he is the only way for people to truly connect with God, and that real truth and vibrant life find their source in him as well. No one else has ever made such an outlandish statement.

We saw last Thursday that Jesus *didn't* say that all roads lead to him or that sincerity is what counts when it comes to spiritual truths. He is the only way to God and he makes no apology for that.

Truth is what holds so many relationships together. When trust and integrity fail, things fragment rapidly. Because Jesus embodies truth, we can trust him with everything that comes our way in life, including the number of our days. He is utterly reliable and totally trustworthy.

Life that God has designed for us is so much more than dry routine or mere existence. Filled with the Holy Spirit daily, we can enjoy the freedom we've been given as chosen and adopted children of God – sons and daughters of the King. Our sins are forgiven, our shame is banished, our past dealt with, our future assured, and we have the privilege of walking in step with Jesus daily, leaning in to hear his voice and enjoy his presence. We become aware of the beautiful world around us – even though humanity has messed it up – and the outworking of God's plans and purposes, of which we are a privileged part.

We carry Jesus in us, so that his way, his truth and his life can be shared with those who are hurting, broken, bereaved, disappointed, struggling – all who are currently unaware of their created uniqueness and God's heart for them. Jesus is the compass, the foundation and the refreshing the world craves. Perhaps we can share him with someone today.

Thank you, Father, that I need never be ashamed of a life lived rooted in Jesus – the best life of all. Thank you that my way is sure, your truth is unchanging and my life abundant because of Jesus. Amen.

JENNY SANDERS

FRIDAY 23 MAY   **JOHN 15:1–8**

The true vine

'I am the true vine, and my Father is the gardener.' (v. 1, NIV)

This conversation about vines and vineyards took place between Jesus and his disciples in the upper room, after their Passover meal but before they headed out to Gethsemane.

Vineyards were a familiar part of the landscape: characteristic trellises flourishing in neat, parallel rows producing grapes for the table and for winemaking. We see them daily in South Africa, which produces some of the best wines in the world. Grapes provide welcome refreshment in dry and dusty places, but they must be curated and nurtured if they are to reach summer harvest in the best condition. The wine industry could not exist without the workers who carefully and systematically tend the vines under the watchful eye of the winemaker.

Jesus' first miracle was to change water into wine at a wedding, reminding us that he loves parties and celebrations – a contrast to the sombre atmosphere in the upper room that night. When we take Communion, in whichever way our tradition prefers, we remember Jesus' once and for all sacrifice (Hebrews 10:10–18) by sharing broken bread, a symbol of his crucified body, and wine that serves as a symbol of his blood, representing the price of our forgiveness.

Jesus' Father, God, is pictured as the gardener, tending the vine to ensure its health and fruitfulness. Read the passage again and you'll find that healthy branches need pruning, while ones that don't produce fruit are removed and discarded. Either way, there's a cutting process that is uncomfortable for the branch.

Walking a life of faith with Jesus isn't always easy. God is shaping us to be more like Jesus. He needs to prune our selfish, old, pre-Jesus habits to see us grow and mature spiritually. He longs for us to flourish, not feel condemned. We can trust this gardener absolutely.

Am I willing to trust God and let him shape me, even though it may sometimes be painful? Being part of his family (the vine) makes this possible.

JENNY SANDERS

SATURDAY 24 MAY JOHN 15:5–17

Connection is critical

'I am the vine; you are the branches.' (v. 5, NIV)

When winemakers talk about a vine, they mean the whole plant. It's difficult to differentiate between the leaves and the branches; the entire shrub is referred to as 'the vine'. By using this imagery, Jesus emphasised the importance of connection, including us as part of himself.

Healthy relationships require good connections. The strongest, most intimate relationships we have are those we invest in. We prioritise them, work hard to communicate well, listen attentively, respond appropriately and express our affection in ways that are meaningful for the other person. Our spiritual relationship is no different.

Prioritising time to speak to and hear from God is important if we want to pursue him, go deeper with him and improve our spiritual health. Reading the Bible and praying are not obligations, but opportunities to enjoy him. The Holy Spirit is the wonderful third person of the Trinity who, unbound by geography, lives within us, empowers us and helps us tune in to God's voice. Through Jesus we can connect with God directly; we no longer require a priest or intermediary. We can come to God confidently, assured that he welcomes us with open arms (Hebrews 4:16).

James 4:8 says: 'Come near to God and he will come near to you' – a reminder that this is not a one-way relationship. We are loved and cherished. It's astonishing to think that the God who created the universe enjoys spending time with us and relishes our company.

If we remain well connected with Jesus, the fruit of his character will grow naturally in our lives and draw others to him. Fruitfulness is the natural outcome of a healthy vine and an indication of good connection within the plant. Being branches of this vine is a wonderful birthright for the children of God.

Thank you, Father, for the privilege of being part of your family. I'm so grateful that I can talk to you at any time and enjoy you anywhere, knowing that your favour rests on me. Amen.

JENNY SANDERS

Amos: from shepherd to prophet

Amy Boucher Pye writes…

Buckle up, friends, as we engage with the book of Amos this week and later in August, because we'll be reading a strongly worded judgement against God's people. We will find a glimmer of hope at the end of the book, a promise to God's people that he'll restore them and repair their broken walls (Amos 9:11); but before that we have to face God's disappointment over their waywardness. As we read and ponder the actions of these beloved but disloyal people from centuries ago, we're also welcomed to respond to God's gentle invitation to examine our own hearts, minds and actions.

However, it's not all gloom and the wearing of hairshirts. One of my friends, fellow writer Tanya Marlow, loves the advocacy she sees in this book with God looking out for the poor, oppressed and victimised. He won't let grievous sins go unnoticed; he will hold the wrongdoers to account.

For context, Amos writes around the same time as fellow prophets Micah and Hosea, and as we'll see in our first reading, he's a shepherd who comes from Judah in the south.* He's speaking to the wealthier northern kingdom of Israel, the people who split off from Judah some 150 years previously. The current king of Israel, Jeroboam II, may have been presiding over prosperity, but the people were becoming increasingly obsessed with idols and false worship while ignoring the poor and the oppressed. Amos addresses this setting of plenty with God's message that is designed to wake them up and prod them to return to him.

God loved his people so much that he didn't want to leave them in their complacency. Nor does he want us to fall into a false sense of satisfaction with our lives. We too can examine our hearts and our motives, asking God to draw us closer to him as we share how we may have let him down. Know that God always rushes towards us in love when we turn to him.

I hope you find encouragement through digging into one of the perhaps more skipped-over prophets and his message of passion and obedience to the God he served.

---

*In writing these notes I drew on several Bible commentaries, finding the most help from the *NIV Application Commentary: Hosea/Amos/Micah* by Gary V. Smith (Zondervan, 2001).

SUNDAY 25 MAY   **AMOS 1:1–8**

Champion for the weak

The words of Amos, one of the shepherds of Tekoa – the vision he saw concerning Israel two years before the earthquake, when Uzziah was king of Judah and Jeroboam son of Jehoash was king of Israel.
(v. 1, NIV)

As I mentioned in the introduction, Amos was a shepherd, not someone used to entering the king's court. Amos wasn't born into this life of delivering messages of judgement, but when called he obeyed God and left his fig trees and sheep to do so. He travelled north to the kingdom of Israel, where the people's hearts were being dulled by prosperity and wealth. Perhaps they thought, why worry about the downtrodden when the pomegranates are plentiful and the feasts abound? And why trouble ourselves with the exacting demands of Yahweh when we can more easily please the two golden idols?

Amos records the words of the living God, the one who created these wayward people and continued to love them, even though they had turned from him. Amos allowed his life to be completely disrupted so that God's message would be heard and heeded. God didn't want his people to continue in their debauchery or their indifference to his kingdom of life, light and truth, so Amos delivered the message of woe.

As we will see again over the next few days, Amos' vision outlines the sins of Israel's neighbours and then those of Israel itself. God first pinpoints the wrongdoing of those closest to Israel geographically. If we look at these places on a map, we see God moving inward from the outside edge of a circle before he reaches Israel with his judgement. 'I will send fire,' the Lord says (v. 4); 'I will break down… I will destroy…' (v. 5). Those committing the horrible injustices of taking people captive and selling them on as slaves (v. 6) will be held to account.

We might find Amos' message difficult to read, but we can feel reassured that evil won't always reign.

Lord God, help me to sense your nudges in my life and your calling upon me, that I might respond faithfully and fully, even as Amos did. Amen.

AMY BOUCHER PYE

MONDAY 26 MAY   **AMOS 1:9—2:3**

The sins of a neighbour

This is what the Lord says: 'For three sins of Edom, even for four, I will not relent. Because he pursued his brother with a sword and slaughtered the women of the land, because his anger raged continually and his fury flamed unchecked, I will send fire.' (vv. 11–12, NIV)

'For three sins of [Britain, or enter your country's name here], even for four, I will not relent,' says the Lord. There's something about hearing this repeated proclamation with the name of our own country included that cuts to the heart. 'Won't the Lord have mercy on us?' we wonder. But when we observe the sins of our homelands – the greed, corruption, squandering of resources, ignoring of what is important – we might agree with God's frustration over the wrongdoing of our nation. And of those countries closest to Israel.

For instance, Tyre (like Gaza as we saw yesterday in verse 6) 'sold whole communities of captives' (v. 9) and Edom not only killed family members but also decimated women (v. 11). The violence of Ammon to the most vulnerable – the pregnant women – is unspeakable (v. 13). God becomes fed up with the bloodshed and atrocities.

The tight structure of Amos' oracles, including the repeated refrains ('for three sins, even for four'), would have led the audience, the Israelites, to believe that God was pronouncing judgement on the neighbouring nations. They would have anticipated the words of love God had for them, his chosen people, but as we will see tomorrow, this is not how he responds. He judges the sins of their neighbours, but he doesn't hold back from judging their wrongdoing either.

Today, as you consider these neighbours from long ago, why not spend some time praying for a country or two near to you geographically? You could do an online search to find out what has been happening lately as you ask the Spirit to lead and guide you. How God answers the prayers of his people is a joyful and wonderful mystery.

'Do not seek revenge or bear a grudge against anyone among your people, but love your neighbour as yourself. I am the Lord' (Leviticus 19:18).

AMY BOUCHER PYE

TUESDAY 27 MAY AMOS 2:4–16

Judgement on Israel

'For three sins of Israel, even for four, I will not relent. They sell the innocent for silver, and the needy for a pair of sandals. They trample on the heads of the poor as on the dust of the ground and deny justice to the oppressed.' (vv. 6–7, NIV)

As we learned yesterday, God's people would feel bolstered by his pronouncements against their neighbours because they knew God was looking out for them. But now Amos delivers God's damning words to both Judah and Israel. His words to Israel are tougher and longer than those to their neighbours. After all, they have been given the privilege and responsibility of being God's people. As they squander this birthright, he shares his disappointment and the consequences of their actions.

As you read through the judgement on Israel, notice that Amos groups it with two emphases. The first is that God's people have abused the weak (vv. 6–8). They discard a human person for the price of a new piece of footwear (v. 6) and the men in the same family have sex with the same woman (v. 7). This was probably not consensual on the woman's part – Amos may have been speaking of a father and son each forcing a female slave to sleep with them – not activity that God was pleased with.

The second group has to do with how God had rescued his people in the past (vv. 9–12). Had they forgotten his deliverance of their ancestors out of Egypt (v. 10)? How he removed the threat of the people already living in the land (vv. 9–10)? They quickly seemed to move on from what God had done for them.

Consequently, in verse 13, God shares what will happen because his people turned from him. When God delivers his judgement, even the bravest and strongest 'will flee naked on that day' (v. 16).

As we consider this stark and painful situation, ponder how far God would go to rectify evil, namely sending his Son Jesus to be the perfect sacrifice for sin.

Loving God, you hate sin and evil. Thank you that believing in you means that your Spirit fills me and helps me to put my wrongdoing behind me. Amen.

AMY BOUCHER PYE

WEDNESDAY 28 MAY AMOS 3:1–8

Cause and effect

Hear this word, people of Israel, the word the Lord has spoken against you – against the whole family I brought up out of Egypt: 'You only have I chosen of all the families of the earth; therefore I will punish you for all your sins.' (vv. 1–2, NIV)

'With great power comes great responsibility' goes the proverb popularised by Spiderman. Amos, however, delivers God's heartfelt pronouncement of this truth with examples rooted in ordinary life. God chose these particular people – they were the *only* ones he knew intimately – and saved them from oppression in Egypt (vv. 1–2). But they sinned and thus he must punish them.

We see a cause-and-effect series of statements in the rest of this section. Notice how in revealing the chain of events, Amos chooses examples that resonate with those listening, such as the lion growling only when there is prey nearby (v. 4) or a trap staying silent when nothing gets caught in it (v. 5). God's people, Amos is saying, have brought this judgement on themselves.

This oracle also includes an affirmation that Amos is God's prophet (v. 7). The people may have scoffed at him; after all, he was a mere shepherd, but he was speaking on behalf of the lion who was roaring, and yes, the correct response was fear (v. 8).

When we read through God's conclusions over his wayward people and the consequences of their actions, we might move too quickly to the saving love of Jesus on the cross. We do have this amazing gift and are washed clean of our sins when we believe in him, but do we use salvation as a form of cheap grace? That is, do we keep on sinning without seeking God's help to stop because we know that he will forgive us?

I welcome you to open your heart and mind before God, asking him to show you where you have strayed from his ways, that not only might you be fully washed clean of any wrongdoing but also grow in godliness in turning away from sin.

'If we claim to be without sin, we deceive ourselves… If we confess our sins, he is faithful and just and will forgive us our sins and purify us from all unrighteousness' (1 John 1:8–9).

AMY BOUCHER PYE

THURSDAY 29 MAY   **AMOS 3:9—4:3**

Cows of Bashan

'Hear this and testify against the descendants of Jacob,' declares the Lord, the Lord God Almighty. 'On the day I punish Israel for her sins, I will destroy the altars of Bethel; the horns of the altar will be cut off and fall to the ground.' (vv. 13–14, NIV)

As Amos continues to share God's disgust with his people's sin and failings, he turns to welcoming Israel's enemies to come and witness their humiliation (v. 9). In their culture, this act of revealing their sins to their neighbours would have felt deeply shameful. But that's how far they had strayed from God and his ways.

We might read verse 12 and shudder at its visual nature, with the images of bones or an ear remaining from a lion's prey. What we might not realise is how this analogy is rooted in Israelite law. Shepherds who were caring for another person's flock were required to return to the owner the bits of a sheep that had been mauled by a lion or other wild animal; this would prove that they hadn't stolen the sheep (see Exodus 22:10–13). This visual language about a subject that Amos knew well would have resonated deeply with those hearing the words of judgement.

God doesn't spare the errant women either. He sees how the 'cows of Bashan' oppress those less fortunate than themselves and won't let it continue. Why all of this judgement? The reason is clear: 'The Sovereign Lord has sworn by his holiness' (4:2). It is because in God there is no sin that he cannot tolerate his people living with such debauchery and with cruel actions against those who have less than they do.

The gift of the Holy Spirit in those who believe in God will help us avoid such outrageous wrongdoing. Nevertheless, we can come before God and ask him to reveal any self-deception or unconfessed sin that is lurking within our hearts. He loves to purify us and make us clean.

'But who can discern their own errors? Forgive my hidden faults. Keep your servant also from wilful sins; may they not rule over me. Then I will be blameless, innocent of great transgression' (Psalm 19:12–13).

AMY BOUCHER PYE

FRIDAY 30 MAY   **AMOS 4:4–8**

Sin yet more

'Go to Bethel and sin; go to Gilgal and sin yet more. Bring your sacrifices every morning, your tithes every three years. Burn leavened bread as a thank-offering and brag about your freewill offerings – boast about them, you Israelites, for this is what you love to do,' declares the Sovereign Lord. (vv. 4–5, NIV)

My children have been brought up in Britain and are both fully versed in banter and irony. Me, having grown up in America, am not. Thus, they will roll their eyes or have to clarify when something feels obtuse or mocking to me. This form of expression goes back centuries and is one Amos fully employs when he tells the Israelites to continue in their sinning. Go to Bethel and Gilgal, he says, holy places where they offer sacrifices, 'and sin yet more' (v. 4). Did you read 'and sin no more' instead of 'and sin yet more'? I keep reading the former, which is what we're used to in the Bible, but here God wants to catch their attention and so switches the form. After all, he says, this is what you love doing (v. 5).

Even though God withdrew his blessing on them, they kept on with their evil deeds and didn't return to the Lord. They lacked bread and rain, but even extreme hunger and thirst weren't enough to help them repent and come back to God. What would it take?

What returns us to God, bringing us to our knees in repentance? As much as I don't enjoy suffering, when I'm in pain I certainly do seek God's love, guidance and presence. Often when I'm wondering about those closest to me and what they are enduring (said children, for instance), I cry out to God on their behalf. My desire for them to be released from the hurts and suffering they endure takes me straight before our loving parent.

May we be those who love to do the things of God, offering not empty sacrifices but our tender hearts, yearning to serve him and others.

'You do not delight in sacrifice, or I would bring it; you do not take pleasure in burnt offerings. My sacrifice, O God, is a broken spirit; a broken and contrite heart you, God, will not despise' (Psalm 51:16–17).

AMY BOUCHER PYE

SATURDAY 31 MAY   **AMOS 4:9–13**

Return to God

He who forms the mountains, who creates the wind, and who reveals his thoughts to mankind, who turns dawn to darkness, and treads on the heights of the earth – the Lord God Almighty is his name (v. 13, NIV).

'You haven't returned to me.' Again and again, through Amos, God reminds his people that they've strayed and haven't returned to the one who created them, he who made a loving covenant with them (vv. 6, 8, 9, 10, 11). Each time before he makes this statement, he shares one of the punishments that he laid out in previous generations in his law (see Leviticus 26). He has taken away food (v. 6), rain (v. 7), crops (v. 9) and life (v. 10), and he has overthrown them (v. 11). Hearing that they've fallen short of the law – that which God wanted to write on to their hearts – should have made them repent.

We're so used to seeing God as loving and kind, full of compassion and overflowing with forgiveness, that to read this litany of consequences more than makes us take pause. 'Who is this angry God?' we think. And yet, if we probe deeply, we see the hurt and disappointment of the one who loves his people. He hasn't given up on them with complete indifference but loves them enough to allow them to experience the consequences of their actions.

As you think back over what you've read this week, which images and thoughts have stayed with you? Perhaps you could skim back over the days, reminding yourself of God's continual disappointment with his prosperous people as expressed by this shepherd turned prophet. You might want to ask yourself, if you're enjoying a time of plenty, how you can avoid the trap of the wealthy Israelites and continue to give God thanks and all the glory? If you're in a season of suffering or pain, what difference does it make that God refuses to let sins go unnoticed?

Ever-loving God, help me not to harden my heart either in times of plenty or times of challenge. I look to you for help and hope, and I affirm that all good things come from you. Amen.

AMY BOUCHER PYE

Mountains and valleys

Jen Baker writes…

Years ago, I was told: 'The good news about a valley season is that the mountaintop soon follows. The bad news is that if you are on the mountaintop there will be a valley season up ahead!' For many years I lived according to these words, vacillating between mountains and valleys, ups and downs. I believed life was a ship subject to the waves of an endless ocean, trying not to capsize on the bad days and enjoying the views on the good ones. I've since changed my belief. Life experience and 35 years as a Christian has shown me the tremendous authority we have over our seasons, proving they are rarely straightforward and fully beyond our control.

A different metaphor would be one of train tracks – one side of the track represents the good happening in one's life and the other side all that is bad. We travel both tracks simultaneously, both joy and sorrow moving us forward. The past five years have proven this metaphor to be surprisingly accurate. Facing a worldwide pandemic brought with it a trauma from which many are still recovering. At the same time, in many places the worldwide church is seeing an increased hunger for something authentic to believe in from those outside the church and seeing miracles and a passion for Jesus increasing as a result.

The Bible is replete with mountain and valley stories and encounters. From sacrificing one's son and preaching to the multitudes on the heights of mountains to fighting giants and defeating hopelessness in the valleys, both give us numerous lessons whatever our season of life.

Take a moment to consider your current season. Would your primary address be a mountaintop or have you found yourself setting up camp in the valleys? Can you see clearly into your future or has the darkness hindered your ability to run the race with confidence like you once did?

Give yourself space this month to examine, enjoy and engage with the scriptures. If you've previously said life is a rollercoaster of ups and downs, consider a new declaration – one that steps away from uncontrollable highs and lows to more of a linear journey filled with learning points and changing landscapes. This journey allows you to step off, explore and step back on when you're ready. It's your train; enjoy the ride.

SUNDAY 1 JUNE   **EXODUS 19:1–20**

Up and down

The Lord came down on Mount Sinai, to the top of the mountain. And the Lord called Moses to the top of the mountain, and Moses went up. (v. 20, ESV)

Mountaintop experiences are often equated with the best of times, yet how many of us know life is never as straightforward as that? This is poignantly demonstrated early in Moses' leadership journey, when he climbs up Mount Sinai to meet a living God who has come down to speak with him.

At the pinnacle of this mountain Moses had a private audience with the Creator, yet one that carried with it a fair share of challenges. While the Israelites stood on the safety of the sidelines, Moses scaled heights, rocks and barriers several times to meet with God. He experienced an enviable holy encounter, but his role as leader of the Israelites brought with it enormous stress physically, emotionally and mentally (see Exodus 18).

So, how would you describe your current season: mountaintop or valley? As I mentioned in the introduction, the last several years have found many of us navigating both seasons at once. Being pulled out of routine and bouncing between joy and sorrow often compels us away from the safety of the sidelines on to a pathway seeking answers. We cannot demand a response from God (been there, tried that!) but we can position ourselves to go higher and hear instructions possibly not audible in a valley of noise and confusion. This takes time and effort. It involves stepping away from people's demands and choosing to go beyond the borders of the familiar to the heights of the unknown.

If the Father called you out of the chaos and into the cloud today, what instructions would you be hoping to receive? Over these next few weeks, set aside time to draw near to God with expectation and a blank page ready to record whatever you hear.

Lord, I'm handing you the pen and eagerly waiting to see what you will write. Give me ears to hear and eyes to see what you are saying in this season. Thank you for meeting me on my mountain. Amen.

JEN BAKER

MONDAY 2 JUNE   **GENESIS 22:1–19**

Go high to let go

Then he reached out his hand and took the knife to slay his son. But the angel of the Lord called out to him from heaven, 'Abraham! Abraham!' 'Here I am,' he replied. (vv. 10–11, NIV)

Did Abraham act in faith or foolishness? It's a debate we've heard over the years with the world screaming child abuse and the church heralding great faith. In Hebrews 11 it says that Abraham believed God could raise his son from the dead. His obedience embodies the truth that faith is foolishness to those who don't believe, while also prophetically paving the way for another Son's sacrifice a few thousand years later.

Recently I watched the film *His Only Son*, which depicts Abraham and Isaac's journey, giving us insight into the possible struggles faced on their walk up the mountain. Time can be a gift or a weight depending upon our circumstances. For Abraham, I imagine it was a bit of both. He had hours to converse with his son while increasingly feeling the weight of each step pulling him away from the decision to let go.

Have you ever experienced a 'Mount Moriah' – that place when God asks something of you that seems impossible to release? It might be a child, dream, desire, spouse or possession. Continuing is no longer an option, while sacrificing feels too great a burden. For me, it was letting go of the dream of having children. I'm now 54 years old, never married, with no children. In my wildest imagination I never thought this story would be my narrative, but it is and I have walked every step of that painful journey.

I've often needed to climb this mountain of surrender with faith, tears, pain, sacrifice, hope and trust. It's been excruciatingly painful at times, yet it's there I've met Jehovah Jireh (provider) in ways I didn't expect. If God is calling you to a mountain of release, climb with courage, because the outcome may be far greater than you imagine.

If you can, watch the film His Only Son *(free online) and consider how you might have responded if you were Abraham. What is God teaching you about surrender through his obedience?*

JEN BAKER

TUESDAY 3 JUNE 1 SAMUEL 17:1–50

Small and significant

Reaching into his bag and taking out a stone, he slung it and struck the Philistine on the forehead. The stone sank into his forehead, and he fell face down on the ground. (v. 49, NIV)

I'm a girl who loves her make-up, stilettos and hazelnut latte, but what many people don't know is that I grew up in mid-western America so I'm also a girl who loves to target practise with a pistol! There's something satisfying about hitting the bullseye knowing the (metaphorical) enemy has been taken down with one shot.

David was a castaway in the eyes of his family yet a king in the eyes of heaven. (As an aside, the lens through which we see ourselves is critical to the battles we are facing, so choose wisely.) In this well-known story, we find David in a valley fighting a giant others refused to face. I remember visiting the Valley of Elah many years ago on a trip to Israel and gathering five smooth stones while imagining my personal giants falling after one well-placed shot.

David's authority and confidence shines through this story (vv. 45–47). He knows his victory will never come from size but significance. Which do you focus on in battle: its size or your significance? How we answer that question is critical to future victories. The truth is we are children of God, carrying an authority given to us by heaven. I love what one preacher said recently, 'One third of us is wall-to-wall Holy Ghost!'

Our heavenly Father calls us royalty, Jesus prays for us continually and the Spirit counsels us repeatedly. Therefore, if you find yourself in a valley right now, pick up the five stones of identity, authority, scripture, worship and prayer. Get the enemy in your sights and believe there is a bullseye waiting to be hit and a giant about to fall. You may feel small, but in Christ you are more than significant.

Lord, thank you that I carry every weapon needed to remove any enemy I face. I choose to boldly declare, as David did, that you will deliver me through the authority I carry in Jesus' name. Amen.

JEN BAKER

WEDNESDAY 4 JUNE   **2 SAMUEL 15:13–30; LUKE 21:37–38**

High and hidden

Each day Jesus was teaching at the temple, and each evening he went out to spend the night on the hill called the Mount of Olives.
(Luke 21:37, NIV)

The Mount of Olives is mentioned numerous times in scripture as a location both for sorrow and celebration. Yesterday we saw David in a valley, but today we find him weeping on this mountain. King David is fleeing from a son who was seeking to steal the throne. He finds himself traversing an emotional road he would never have imagined as he wept over a child's rejection and rebellion. The Mount of Olives proves a useful place for his emotions to pour out until sobs eventually become worship (v. 32).

Luke tells us that the Mount of Olives was a special place for Jesus, and it is here that we see Jesus praying and weeping before his arrest (Luke 22). Drops of blood began falling from his brow as he hid himself among the rocks and cried out amid the darkness.

When those closest to you have caused you pain, where do you go? Your Mount of Olives may not be a physical mountain, but having a place you can retreat to when life overwhelms you is of great importance in the life of faith. It might be a prayer chair, favourite cafe, up a literal mountain or out in nature. Over the years my space has changed from a specific corner chair to a seaside walk along the coastline. At times I've been limited to my bed and other days a hotel room is as good as it gets.

Our high place doesn't have to be fancy, but it helps if it is familiar. We need to feel safe so that we can freely pour out our hearts to the Father, without edit or shame, knowing in joy or sorrow we will never be rejected.

Though not exhaustive, here are further mentions of the Mount of Olives in scripture: Ezekiel 11:23, Mark 13:3–4, Luke 24:50–52; Acts 1:12. What theme(s) do you find as you read these verses?

JEN BAKER

THURSDAY 5 JUNE   **PSALM 23**

The shepherd in the shadows

Even though I walk through the darkest valley, I will fear no evil, for you are with me; your rod and your staff, they comfort me. (v. 4, NIV)

I am guessing 'the darkest valley' might be one of the most well-known valleys in the Bible. It may not be a physical valley, but its description carries with it a foreboding sense of steep cliffs either side and a sunless gorge down below. It feels impossible to escape, which makes the isolation that much greater. Seasons of physical pain, broken hearts, unbearable sorrow and unanswerable questions find us walking this valley at one time or another throughout our lives.

One of the most beautiful truths about this valley is that it is where you find a shepherd waiting in the shadows. Holding a staff of comfort, he invites us to dine at a table off limits to the enemies we are fleeing. This famous psalm bookends the grief by opening with words of provision and restoration while ending with reminders of goodness, mercy and enduring faithfulness. This is not a valley to be feared but one where peace can be found. Here I'm protected from my enemy, provided for by my Saviour and empowered for eternity. This is not a valley to avoid in fear but one to embrace in faith.

When you find the enemy speaking louder than you can worship, chasing faster than you can run and becoming more devious than you can defeat, turn to this valley. Go down into the hidden, sunless, quiet place where your shepherd longs to meet you. Because while you've been running, he's been preparing, and as you've been looking back, he's been making provision to carry you forward. The chair is pulled out, will you sit down?

Lord, thank you for meeting me in my darkest places, preparing a table arranged just for me. I choose to look for you in the shadows, seeing you step forward in love, provision, mercy and faithfulness. Amen.

JEN BAKER

FRIDAY 6 JUNE   **DEUTERONOMY 32:48–52**

A higher perspective

'Therefore, you will see the land only from a distance; you will not enter the land I am giving to the people of Israel'. (v. 52, NIV)

These verses feel cruel to me. Moses endured years of abuse as he led millions of whining people around in circles in the wilderness until the generation who had disobeyed God were gone. He had one bad day and in a fit of anger rebelled against God's command. As a result, he was permitted to see the promised land only from a distance. Seems a little harsh!

I realise there are theological reasons for the severity of the punishment and leadership is held to a standard that is higher than others, but I still have empathy for our friend Moses. At the very least these verses remind me that obedience is not a small matter to the Lord and partial obedience is not acceptable.

However, what I find beautiful is that the Lord invited Moses up on Mount Nebo to show him the next generation's future. Moses had done his part, not perfectly but faithfully, and was nearing the end of his life. He wouldn't take this generation into the land, but years later he would stand with Jesus on the same soil he now spies from a distance.

Higher perspectives often bring today's clarity and tomorrow's foresight. Have you ever been overlooked for a job only to find a better one arise a few years later? Or in hindsight been grateful for the broken heart because of who you met around the corner? What we cannot understand today may not be explained tomorrow, but going higher allows us the opportunity to see from a vantage point that which our self-centered world cannot see. The bottom line is that when I stop holding God hostage to an explanation, I open myself up to receive blessings and opportunities impossible to see from my current vantage point.

When has the Lord protected you even if you didn't see it at the time? How does that help you view your current circumstances? Read Proverbs 3:5–6 and thank him for his faithfulness over your life!

JEN BAKER

SATURDAY 7 JUNE   **1 KINGS 19:1–18**

A still small voice

And after the earthquake a fire, but the Lord was not in the fire. And after the fire the sound of a low whisper. (v. 12, ESV)

Elijah experienced a rough few months. He had taken on 400 prophets of Baal in a test of 'whose God is more powerful' and won by a landslide (or more accurately by fire) which found him on the wrong side of Jezebel. She vowed to see Elijah killed, which necessitated a swift escape. From his time on Mount Carmel to his arrival at Mount Horeb he had not only fled for his life but also traversed several hundred miles. He was weary, weakened and a bit whiney after such a traumatic and exhausting season.

I don't know about you, but I've been there. You know those seasons when a potential victory is surrounded by a battle so intense you wonder if the victory was really worth it? Those are the days I dream of running away to a deserted island, just me and my coffee. In those seasons I have longed for a word from heaven (accompanied by writing on the wall) giving me direction out of the pain, fear and confusion. Maybe you've also noticed that the times when we need to hear from God the most are often when he speaks the least? It was on this mountain where Elijah experienced power, noise and movement through wind, earthquake and fire, but the one thing he truly sought – the voice of God – was nowhere to be found.

It took a low whisper to speak volumes. The NRSV translates 'low whisper' as 'sheer silence'. To hear a whisper, one must be very close to the one who is speaking. Imagine the voice of God so near to Elijah's ear that what was nearly silent became surprisingly clear. If you find yourself in a season of running in fear, I encourage you to forget the coffee and seek silence over signs.

Lord, thank you for speaking volumes in your own unique way. Forgive me for the times I've limited the ways I hear you. Help my spiritual ears be attuned to your voice, loud or quiet, in this season. Amen.

JEN BAKER

SUNDAY 8 JUNE   **MATTHEW 5**

A mountain of truth

'Do not think that I have come to abolish the Law or the Prophets; I have not come to abolish them but to fulfil them.' (v. 17, NIV)

We cannot talk about mountains and valleys without visiting one of the most well-known Bible passages, the sermon on the mount. Many years ago, I visited Israel and our guide pointed out what many thought was the location for Jesus' most famous sermon. It was awe inspiring to look at the landscape, imagining Jesus teaching thousands of people while overlooking the Sea of Galilee.

This is the longest running sermon by Jesus found in the Bible and one packed with too much truth to expound in a daily devotional. Jesus breaks all the preaching rules with its length, depth and breadth, but my goodness is this a sermon worth reading on repeat for the ages! At the beginning we find Jesus declaring that he's not trying to do away with what was old, he is fulfilling and releasing the new. Truth does that; it sets us free (John 8:31–32) by challenging us to revisit old mindsets with fresh perspective.

Perhaps there is a person or situation you need to view through the lens of this sermon? Have you held anyone captive to an old identity, refusing to give them the benefit of the doubt when they say that they've changed? Are you trusting in your works instead of God's grace? Have you found yourself gossiping about your enemies instead of praying for them?

This mountain challenges us to our core because it puts a spotlight on sin and filters our motives through the lens of our Father's love. Take time to read Matthew 5—7 slowly, contemplatively and honestly as you allow the Holy Spirit to highlight what he'd like to say to you on this mountain of truth. I'm guessing you may find yourself in awe, departing the mountain with a new view and fresh freedom.

Lord, as I read these chapters, please show me where I need correcting, loving, freeing and/or releasing. Thank you for being a safe space to honestly examine my heart. I trust your love to lead me into all truth. Amen.

JEN BAKER

MONDAY 9 JUNE HOSEA 2:14–23

A door of hope

There I will give her back her vineyards, and will make the Valley of Achor a door of hope. There she will respond as in the days of her youth, as in the day she came up out of Egypt. (v. 15, NIV)

The Valley of Achor is a place that symbolises severe trouble or affliction. It was here that Achan and his family were destroyed due to Achan's sin (Joshua 7), and it became associated with judgement and punishment. Hundreds of years later the prophet Hosea revisits this valley and declares what had once symbolised death would now become a door. This is a beautiful example of grace redeeming, reforming and restoring.

Have you put a 'do not enter' sign in front of any personal valleys due to sin, shame or painful memories? Though forgiveness has covered the deep furrow of shame our wrong choices have created, we still prefer to keep our sins hidden. We cannot change our past but what if we could rename it? One beautiful truth about our Father is that he relishes restoration, not reminders.

Let's take a journey together for a moment. Imagine you are walking through your Valley of Achor but you are carrying a bag of seeds. You notice these seeds sprouting as soon as you step away, leaving a trail of flowers behind you. As it's your valley, you get to choose where the flowers lay and how many you leave behind. Over which memories would you plant them? How many would you leave? What colours would they become?

For anyone stuck in a valley of past pain, I implore you to let the God of hope restore your valley to a new name. How do you do that? Intentionally drop seeds of hope, forgiveness and grace over your valley until the meadow becomes a door of hope welcoming you into a fresh perspective and renewed expectancy.

Lord, thank you for the seeds of truth given to us in the Bible. Please show me which scriptures are my seeds of hope. I choose to walk in courage as I plant them in faith, expecting a great harvest. Amen.

JEN BAKER

TUESDAY 10 JUNE **MATTHEW 17:1–13**

Place of encounter

While he was still speaking, a bright cloud covered them, and a voice from the cloud said, 'This is my Son, whom I love; with him I am well pleased. Listen to him!' (v. 5, NIV)

I clearly remember a time when I faced a big decision and my father told me that he believed in me. He went on to speak a deeply personal sentence that he'd never said before, which made my heart grow about three sizes in three seconds. Conversations can transform lives, especially in seasons of great change and uncertainty.

Interestingly, the same words of affirmation seen in the scripture above were spoken ten chapters earlier (Matthew 3:17), immediately after Jesus' baptism. Those at his baptismal service heard the bellowing sounds of heaven's approval before Jesus had even started his public ministry. Fast forward three years and Jesus is rapidly approaching the end of his ministry when the same words of love and affirmation are spoken by his Father, interrupting Peter's awkwardly inappropriate suggestion of a building project. Jesus' transfiguration also happened on this mountain, where he encountered a surprise visit from Elijah and Moses. Have you ever wondered what they talked about? What words of advice do you give someone about to take on the sins of the world?

Do you know anyone stepping into a task that feels daunting or facing a season of change? It might be the joy of new life or the pain of saying goodbye, the beginning of a journey or the end. Words are important at the best of times but carry greater impact at the worst of times. If you are uncertain what to say in the moment, remember these fathers. Both the heavenly Father and my earthly father show us what to do when we don't know what to do: speak life, speak love.

Brainstorm ways to encourage those you know facing a big change. Perhaps you can write them a letter, give them a phone call or take them for a coffee. Ask the Lord for wisdom, and follow where he leads.

JEN BAKER

WEDNESDAY 11 JUNE   **PSALM 84**

Valley of lament

Blessed are those whose strength is in you, whose hearts are set on pilgrimage. As they pass through the Valley of Baka, they make it a place of springs; the autumn rains also cover it with pools. They go from strength to strength, till each appears before God in Zion.
(vv. 5–7, NIV)

In this psalm of pilgrimage, we encounter the Valley of Baka. The psalm declares a longing for the courts of heaven while equally lamenting the long road stretching ahead. We can hear the psalmist's desire for the presence of God, yet he knows as joyful as heaven's glory will be, he must first endure the trials of earth.

I recently experienced a time when I seemed to weep for days. The pain felt unbearable and, even worse, unending. If there was a light at the end of the tunnel I was definitely in the middle, because all I could see was darkness, confusion and hopelessness. In these seasons we lament. We cry out to God in raw honesty, refusing to censor the senses and mute the mutiny. God can handle our pain and if we feel like quitting, yelling or rebelling there's freedom to follow through; God knows it all anyway.

Baka can be translated 'weeping', 'drought' or 'dryness caused by trouble and vexation'. Whether a literal place or not, it's clearly not a desired destination. This is specifically a valley you pass through and one which, one day, you will see transformed from a dry valley to a place of springs.

If you are in a season of lament allow yourself the freedom to feel, speak, be honest and acknowledge the truth of your circumstances. Then, after you have taken as much time as you need, look around. Begin to smell the spring, see your resilience and regain vision for your future. Often the valley is shorter than we think and home is closer than we know. Trust the lament.

Read Psalm 22 and notice the pattern of lament: address, complaint, request, expression of trust. Use this to inspire your own personal prayer of lament.

JEN BAKER

THURSDAY 12 JUNE 2 CHRONICLES 20

Hold your ground

'You will not have to fight this battle. Take up your positions; stand firm and see the deliverance the Lord will give you, Judah and Jerusalem. Do not be afraid; do not be discouraged. Go out to face them tomorrow, and the Lord will be with you.' (v. 17, NIV)

In nearly 25 years of ministry, I have had several occasions when I felt there was 'a great multitude' coming against me (v. 2, ESV) and I was in a no-way-out valley, surrounded by the enemy. Times like this tend to engage the fight-or-flight mentality and, if I'm honest, flight often yells the loudest. What I love about these verses is that it says Jehoshaphat was alarmed (v. 3), so he prayed and sought the Lord. He didn't flee, whine, moan, plan, gossip, blame or try to bargain his way out of the dilemma. This king knew where his strength lay and it wasn't in riches, position or the size of his army. This raises the question: who or what do you turn to when you feel surrounded?

I'll never forget what God said to me one morning during a particularly challenging season when I knew lies were being spoken and misunderstandings were spreading faster than a virus. I sat at my desk stewing over my circumstances, thinking of all the ways I could justify my actions, when the Lord told me to stay silent. 'Are you kidding me, Lord? Have you confused me with someone else's crisis and missed what they've been saying about me? Surely I should defend myself!' Nope.

In that season I learned that silence is a weapon. God fought for me and the blessings on the other side were beyond what I could have imagined. Jehoshaphat found the same truth in the Valley of Berakah, which means praise. It took days for the Israelites to retrieve the spoils of war they didn't have to fight for. I have learned that God's love is greater than my battle and his victory reaches farther than my bitterness. My main job? Let God do his job.

Lord, thank you for your faithfulness in my life and through this season. I trust you to watch over me, and I choose to worship you until I receive the spoils of war. Amen.

JEN BAKER

FRIDAY 13 JUNE   **GENESIS 8:1–19**

Sitting and waiting

The water receded steadily from the earth. At the end of the hundred and fifty days the water had gone down, and on the seventeenth day of the seventh month the ark came to rest on the mountains of Ararat. (vv. 3–4, NIV)

Mount Ararat is famous for being the resting place of Noah's ark. Here his family and local menagerie lived in their homemade shipping container while waiting for the floods to subside. How frustrating it must have been (let alone odorous) as they waited week after week and month after month, having no idea when the prolonged house move was coming to an end. It's one thing to have a timeline for a stressful season, but it's quite another to have an open-ended battle with no finish line in sight. It reminds me of the beginning of the Covid pandemic, when nobody knew what was happening or for how long our lives would be turned upside down.

While most of us love metaphorical mountaintop seasons, some mountains are meant to hold us in our pain, not lift us to new heights. Have you allowed yourself rest from the worldwide unrest of the last five years? Perhaps the Lord is asking you to step into his ark of peace for a season? If Noah had delayed, he would have been doomed; obedience was paramount for his safety, and it's the same for us.

Rest doesn't have to look like months alone in solitude; it could be a day away in retreat. We are all in different places; those with young children, for example, may find it more difficult to get time away. But even driving an hour or staying overnight at a local hotel can be our Mount Ararat if we allow it to be. The point is to schedule something. Make space for rest and allow yourself to view the storm from a different vantage point. Then one day, when you least expect it, a rainbow of hope will appear and a new season will begin.

Thank you, Lord, for mountains of rest when we are navigating personal storms. Help me to stop trying to leave your safe place before it's time. I declare peace over my mind, heart and home in the name of Jesus. Amen.

JEN BAKER

SATURDAY 14 JUNE   **JOHN 19**

A mountain of freedom

Carrying his own cross, he went out to the place of the Skull (which in Aramaic is called Golgotha). (v. 17, NIV)

The site where Jesus was crucified may not equal the physical size of the mountains Abraham, Noah and Moses faced, but it was a mountain nonetheless. Here is where sin was carried, shame was done away with and freedom was bought. What may have looked like a small mountain to climb became the hardest road any human being would ever walk.

At times our mountains may appear like molehills to the outside world, because nobody knows the sorrows and challenges we face or have faced in our past (Proverbs 14:10). Golgotha shows us that the smallest mountains may carry the greatest breakthroughs. It could be forgiveness offered for the hundredth time, an act of love given to one who used to love you, the choice to speak life when you want to be critical or applying for a job after your kids have left home… the list is endless.

Many years ago, I made what appeared to be an innocuous phone call, but it was anything but safe. On the receiving end was the man who had abused me as a child. To say I was terrified is a vast understatement, but when he answered I found courage (after months of counselling) to say that I forgave him and had been praying that he would know the love of Christ. What I could not have expected was an apology followed by his testimony that a few years prior he had made a commitment to the Lord. He was my brother in Christ!

It took climbing a mountain of fear, hurt and confusion before I understood that facing what held my pain eventually unlocked my freedom. Jesus knows what it feels like to climb hard mountains and walk through deep valleys. Always remember, you'll never walk alone.

Thank you that I never journey alone. You are with me through brambles and darkness, heights and victories. Jesus, I give you my hand to hold as we walk through mountains and valleys now and in the years to come. Amen.

JEN BAKER

What the Bible says about being a man

Chine McDonald writes…

I come from a family of women. I have sisters and no brothers, while my parents have nine sisters between them. When my husband and I found out we were pregnant for the first time, all I could picture was our little girl. So, I was in shock when at our 20-week scan, the sonographer told us we would be having a boy!

After three days of labour, when my son was eventually born, I still didn't quite believe that I could have a son, so seconds after the midwife had taken him away to be checked I asked her: 'Is he definitely a boy?' When the sonographer scanning me during my next pregnancy confirmed that I would be having another boy, I was even more stunned. So much of my identity has been wrapped up in being a woman – a woman who is attempting to live life following Christ. I was very conscious of the shift in mindset and outlook that would be needed for me to bring up boys.

I have spent many years noticing the pressures society places on women, but I have realised there is so much pervasive messaging that attempts to define what a man should be like, too. When I think of what it is to be a man, I too often revert to lazy stereotypes that characterise men in one-dimensional ways, but I have been struck by how much I want my own little boys to be free to grow into the men that God has called them to be.

The Bible is full of examples of what it is to be a man. Sometimes these biblical examples conform to the patriarchal societies in which the scriptures were written, but when I come to the example of Jesus, I see a rich, varied and wonderful example of being a man. Jesus surprised people in so many ways, breaking down the barriers of what society perceived to be right and good. Jesus showed emotion: anger, anxiety, heartbreak. Jesus showed tender compassion to those who were suffering and held nothing back when he perceived hypocrisy or people oppressing others. In Jesus, we have a blueprint for the ultimate man. He is both like and unlike the men we see around us. In so being, Jesus presents us with the variety that there can be in mankind and shows us the freedom we all have to be who we are called to be – fearfully and wonderfully made.

SUNDAY 15 JUNE LUKE 15:11–32

The prodigal father

'So he got up and went to his father. But while he was still a long way off, his father saw him and was filled with compassion for him; he ran to his son, threw his arms round him and kissed him.' (v. 20, NIV)

One of my favourite movie scenes of all time takes place on a station platform in the 1970 film adaptation of E. Nesbit's classic book *The Railway Children*. In it, eldest daughter Bobbie – played by a young Jenny Agutte – runs into the arms of her father, who has been away a long time and emerges through the steam – smiling but stoic – waiting for his daughter's embrace.

Today is Father's Day, and perhaps you can recall the warmth of your own dad's embrace. There may be some people for whom this is something you longed for but never received, or perhaps your father was absent in your life, or his presence was not a positive one. Whatever our personal experiences of our fathers, we all have an idea of what a good father is. In today's passage, the prodigal son is met with the overwhelming love of his father, shown in the extravagance of his compassionate embrace.

In *The Railway Children*, Bobbie runs to her father; in this passage, the father runs to his son. Here, the father represents our heavenly Father. The story tells us that – although we may not feel worthy of love, though we may feel wretched and filled with shame and regret – God loves us. Not reluctantly or begrudgingly because that is how a man is *supposed* to be towards his children, but with arms wide open. C.S. Lewis puts it well when he describes what it feels like to be on the receiving end of God's extravagant love: 'We are embarrassed by the intolerable compliment, by too much love, not too little.'

Father God, thank you for your extravagant love, freely given. Help us to freely give it to others, with the help of your Holy Spirit. Amen.

CHINE MCDONALD

MONDAY 16 JUNE   **JOHN 11:17–36**

How he loved

When Mary reached the place where Jesus was and saw him, she fell at his feet and said, 'Lord, if you had been here, my brother would not have died.' When Jesus saw her weeping… he was deeply moved in spirit and troubled. 'Where have you laid him?' he asked. 'Come and see, Lord,' they replied. Jesus wept. Then the Jews said, 'See how he loved him!' (vv. 32–36, NIV)

Jesus wept. This is the shortest verse in the Bible, yet it is so profound. Reading this verse shatters preconceptions about what a man should be and how a man should behave. I have always been deeply moved by this passage. Jesus' dear friends Mary and Martha are distraught at the death of their brother. You can sense their frustration and deep anguish.

One of the most painful things in life is to experience the death of a loved one. Despite the ultimate hope and faith we might have in God, we still feel the sting of death and the tragedy of grief as we mourn their loss. We are reminded of the brokenness of our world and the fracture that exists in creation.

This passage teaches us that God understands our grief. In Jesus, God became human and walked among us. Jesus – a man – feels deeply and loves his friends deeply. God is so often depicted as a triumphant, warrior-like, all-powerful and stereotypically male God, but Jesus' tears of tenderness show the softness of our loving God, who does not stand apart from our suffering but suffers with us.

Jesus also reflects to us what it is to be human – to love and care for others, to feel each other's pain and share each other's burdens. Knowing that Jesus understands how it feels to be moved by the plight of others, we feel able to share our emotion, knowing that we can find a sense of refuge and safety in the arms of our all-loving God.

God who weeps with us, help us not to be constrained by a fear of judgement for showing our emotions. May we know true freedom in you today. Amen.

CHINE MCDONALD

TUESDAY 17 JUNE   **1 TIMOTHY 4**

The value of godliness

Have nothing to do with godless myths and old wives' tales; rather, train yourself to be godly. For physical training is of some value, but godliness has value for all things, holding promise for both the present life and the life to come. (vv. 7–8, NIV)

Timothy was one of a large group of protégés and coworkers Paul had gathered around him in his ministry. Paul had sent Timothy to Ephesus specifically to confront some of the false teaching that had infiltrated the church there.

A particular problem were the beliefs and behaviours of older men who, influenced by the predominant culture in Rome, made physical exercise their number one priority. Timothy was still young, but Paul recognised the spirit of God in him and his letter both encourages Timothy and sets out Paul's guidance and instruction for the church.

Many of our western cultures today regard physical exercise as a moral good. According to NHS statistics, a higher proportion of men (70%) than women (59%) meet the guidelines for daily exercise. Go into any gym and you will find it predominantly filled with men, often building up muscle strength to conform to the idea of manliness that our culture holds as desirable.

In his letter, Paul doesn't dismiss the value of physical training, but urges the church to prioritise growing in godliness, strengthening their spiritual muscles rather than their temporal, physical ones. It is a reminder to the Jesus followers not to be swayed by the culture around them, which is ephemeral and fleeting, but to look to what is eternal. Spiritual training matters for both this life and the life that is to come.

God who strengthens us, help us today to seek your kingdom, to train ourselves to be more like you, through the help of your Holy Spirit. In Jesus' name. Amen.

CHINE MCDONALD

WEDNESDAY 18 JUNE   MICAH 6:1–8

More than words

He has told you, O man, what is good; and what does the Lord require of you but to do justice, and to love kindness, and to walk humbly with your God? (v. 8, ESV)

This must be one of the most quoted passages in scripture. I even have this verse written on a mug, reminding me as I drink my morning coffee of what God has asked me to do. It is easily quoted, but much harder to live out. It sounds great and, like the rest of the book of Micah, it is written in a poetic form. It rolls off the tongue, but these are more than just nice words. They are extraordinarily difficult challenges for us in our daily lives.

The prophet Micah is one of twelve men known as the 'minor' prophets, who are called such simply because their books are shorter than the 'major' prophets, which include Isaiah, Ezekiel and Jeremiah – the terms 'major' and 'minor' here are not value judgements. As I think about what it is to be a man today, I am reminded of the difficulty men experience when they are judged as inadequate, especially in comparison to other men. So much of human history has been about men fighting over land, attempting to grab power and elevate their sense of status. The desire for power is found at the root of many injustices we see around the world.

In this short but powerful book, Micah is speaking about how displeased God is with the injustice being perpetrated by Israel, but it doesn't end there. Micah ends with hope as he reveals that God's ultimate purpose is to save and restore, not to punish. It is this knowledge of God's ultimate plan that should spur us all – both men and women – to honour God's call for us 'to do justice, to love kindness, and to walk humbly' with him.

Loving God, we pray that we would be people who do not just pay lip service to doing justice but seek to love kindness and to walk humbly with you. Amen.

CHINE MCDONALD

THURSDAY 19 JUNE   **GENESIS 1:24–31**

After God's likeness

Then God said, 'Let Us make man in Our image, according to Our likeness; let them have dominion over the fish of the sea, over the birds of the air, and over the cattle, over all the earth and over every creeping thing that creeps on the earth.' (v. 26, NKJV)

Since the 1980s, much of the discussion around men in academic circles and the media has been around the idea of 'toxic masculinity' – destructive traits traditionally associated with the male of the species, such as misogyny, aggression and forcefulness.

Toxic masculinity also includes the idea that men are emotionally repressed, unable to say how they feel or show any vulnerability. Since much of the world is in a mess and men still rule the world when it comes to global leadership, men are blamed for all that is wrong with the world.

I spend a large part of my life working for equality for women. I am absolutely committed to a fairer world for all – and that includes my sons and my husband. It can be easy to cast a whole group of people in a negative light, without leaving room for the individual characteristics and positive traits that make up a person. Today's passage reminds us that whatever the world might say about us, we are made in God's image.

I like to understand the *imago Dei* as a description of the special 'something' – the X factor, perhaps – that runs through each and every person. It is the sparkle of God's light that exists in us, no matter who we are, and no matter what we have done.

Being made in God's image does not get us off the hook for bad behaviour or exhibiting toxic traits – whether or not our society has conditioned us to think they are how we must behave. The image of God in us leaves room for diversity, wonder and beauty.

Creator God, thank you that you made us in your image. May we remember that we – and everyone we encounter today – has that sparkle that comes only from you. Amen.

CHINE MCDONALD

FRIDAY 20 JUNE LUKE 7:1–9

Say the word

'Lord, don't trouble yourself, for I do not deserve to have you come under my roof. That is why I did not even consider myself worthy to come to you. But say the word, and my servant will be healed'.
(vv. 6–7, NIV)

Today, we meet one of the New Testament's most surprising examples of faith – the Roman centurion, who pleads with Jesus on behalf of his servant who is ill, believing that Jesus will heal him, even from afar. The centurion represents a stereotype of manliness: he's a decorated soldier, he's in charge of many other soldiers, he's a boss.

I recently had one of the most intimidating experiences of my life when I gave a presentation at Sandhurst Military Academy to a room full of generals in the British Army. It was intimidating because of the authority they carried. These uniformed men (they were predominantly male) had been on the frontline serving their country and had made their way to the top in the army. Thousands of soldiers looked to them for guidance and permission. They carried themselves as people who knew the power that they held.

However, in this story, there are so many things about the centurion that turn the idea of what it is to be a man in leadership on its head. He clearly has profound and deep care for his servant and, contrary to many of his colleagues, he is in good relationship with the Jewish leaders. He has a humility that – despite the authority he has – defers to Jesus because he recognises who Jesus is.

This passage also teaches us about the power of faith. The centurion believes that Jesus only has to say the word and his servant will be healed. How many times do we doubt what Jesus can do in our lives or the lives of those around us? I confess I have been guilty of this at times. The centurion's faith, though, is catching. By seeing the faith of those around us, we too can be encouraged to be faith-filled.

All-powerful God, we are sorry for the times when we doubt. Help our unbelief and give us faith as unshakeable as the centurion's. Amen.

CHINE MCDONALD

SATURDAY 21 JUNE ROMANS 12:9–21

Signs of care

Let love be genuine. Abhor what is evil; hold fast to what is good. Love one another with brotherly affection. Outdo one another in showing honour. (v. 9, ESV)

My eldest son's best friend was over for a playdate recently. In those hours together, I got a front-row seat into the world of friendship among six-year-old boys. There were fights and disagreements, the occasional tears of frustration: about what games they should play and in what order, which shows they should watch on the television and what snacks they should have. Similarly, when I watch the little boys in our village school, there is often a lot of rough and tumble – a lot of energy that they seem to constantly need to burn off.

When my son's friend's mum arrived to pick him up, both boys were sad to say goodbye to each other. Despite the bickering and the energy, they embraced each other with a love that brought a tear to my eye. Our boys have not yet been exposed to a world that says men should not show each other 'brotherly affection', as today's passage exhorts.

In the passage, the Greek word *philostorgoi* is used to describe that familiar, comfortable love; a love that is at ease and not-self-conscious. Meanwhile *philadelphia* – brotherly love – describes those familial bonds that cannot be broken despite disagreements. This is how Paul wants the church to show love to each other. It is a love that runs deep, that is found in authentic community. It is a grace-filled love that comes only from the Spirit at work within us, as God's people. This at-ease love, this brotherly affection, is an outpouring of a community of people who genuinely care for one another. This is what the kingdom of God is supposed to be like – for all of us: children, women and men.

Loving God, bind us – the community of believers made in your image – together with love that cannot be broken. Help us be a witness to the world of what it is to love unconditionally. Amen.

CHINE MCDONALD

SUNDAY 22 JUNE   **MATTHEW 21:12–17**

A righteous anger

Jesus entered the temple courts and drove out all who were buying and selling there. He overturned the tables of the money-changers and the benches of those selling doves. 'It is written,' he said to them, '"My house will be called a house of prayer," but you are making it "a den of robbers."' (vv. 12–13, NIV)

For most of my childhood, I thought of Jesus as gentle, meek and mild. In the illustrated children's Bibles that were read to us in Sunday school, a white, blue-eyed Jesus with soft, wavy hair would stand in gardens surrounded by flowers and lambs. He looked quiet and timid. In my child's eye, he looked like someone who – if I were ever to do anything wrong – would look at me with a soft and gentle disappointment, rather than shout in rage. This is why, when I got to the gospel accounts of Jesus overturning the tables of the money-changers in the temple, it did not fit with the image of Jesus I had in my mind. Jesus' childlike gentleness had made him stand out from the dominant idea of what men are supposed to be like, but in this scene, in which Jesus displays his anger, he appears to be acting in a stereotypical way.

However, what we are seeing here is righteous anger towards those who have made God's house a 'den of robbers'. The New Testament accounts of Jesus show him displaying a full range of emotions: joy, love, sarcasm, welcome, fear, anxiety, sadness and, yes, anger. When we are called to follow Christ, God does not require men or women to become passive and emotionless. God does not expect us to be unmoved by injustice – especially towards those who are in need. Our relationship with God means we can bring our whole selves – warts and all – knowing that those characteristics which need to be worked on in us will be so through the help of the Holy Spirit.

God of justice, may we never be unmoved by wrongdoing or injustice. Stir up our hearts that we may work to bring about your kingdom here on earth. Amen.

CHINE MCDONALD

MONDAY 23 JUNE   **1 KINGS 2:1–10**

The ultimate encouragement

When the time drew near for David to die, he gave a charge to Solomon his son. 'I am about to go the way of all the earth,' he said. 'So be strong, act like a man, and observe what the Lord your God requires.' (vv. 1–3, NIV)

It is well-documented that at the end of life, people have the same last messages to pass on to their loved ones. They say sorry, they ask for forgiveness, they themselves forgive and they say, 'I love you.' Former palliative care doctor Kathryn Mannix has written and spoken extensively about a good death involving these tender moments. At the end of life, we want to say what really matters.

In today's passage, King David, who is described as a man after God's own heart (1 Samuel 13:14), knows that he will soon die and, just as Jacob had made his last wishes known to Joseph (Genesis 47:29), he wants to impart his own final messages to his son Solomon. A simple reading of David's instruction may suggest that David is telling his son to do what society so often tells men to do: to 'man up'. He is indeed urging his son to act like a man, but it is an encouragement – a rallying call – to claim the authority of his kingly throne and to protect their people by whatever means necessary.

It seems that this last message David has for his son is for him to have courage. It's the ultimate pep talk before he becomes king. Perhaps this is David's way of showing his love for his son. He does not want his child to be afraid, but to know that whatever challenges he might face, God will be with him.

David's words to Solomon speak to us too. We don't have to fear what lies ahead, because we too have God's promise that he will be with us.

Victorious God, we thank you for the words of encouragement you give us. Help us to have courage to face whatever it is that stands before us today – whether big or small. Amen.

CHINE MCDONALD

TUESDAY 24 JUNE   **DEUTERONOMY 30:11–20**

Under pressure

I have set before you life and death, blessings and curses. Now choose life, so that you and your children may live and that you may love the Lord your God, listen to his voice, and hold fast to him.
(vv. 19–20, NIV)

My husband and I recently went to see *For Black Boys* at a theatre in central London. I had been waiting years to see this play, but though I was excited to get tickets, I also approached the theatre with trepidation. I knew I was in for a heavy evening. The play's full title is *For Black Boys Who Have Considered Suicide When The Hue Gets Too Heavy*.

Based on the choreo-poem *For Colored Girls* by Ntozake Shange, published in the 1970s, *For Black Boys* is a series of monologues and meditations on the joys, pains and challenges of being both black and male. As a mum of two biracial boys, I felt the weight of the pressures placed on boys and men to live up to unachievable standards: to 'man up' when they want to curl up into a ball and shut the world away.

Each of the characters in the play contemplates ending it all because the pressure gets too much. In recent years, suicide has become the leading cause of death for men aged between 35 and 49. The figures are much higher than for women.

This seems to be a taboo topic within the church, but as Christians who believe in a God of hope, we have something to offer into this conversation. It is not just about encouraging men to talk about their feelings. Today's passage might seem simplistic considering the depth of pain that might lead a man to take his own life, but God is not simply asking people to make a choice. The God who commands us to choose life here also asks us to 'listen to his voice, and hold fast to him'. He is inviting people into a relationship with him.

God who speaks, we pray for all those who are suffering from despair and hopelessness today. Break into their hearts and minds, and bring others around them who can support them in their struggles. Amen.

CHINE MCDONALD

WEDNESDAY 25 JUNE   **LUKE 5:12–16**

Time for solitude

Yet the news about him spread all the more, so that crowds of people came to hear him and to be healed of their illnesses. But Jesus often withdrew to lonely places and prayed. (vv. 15–16, NIV)

I love a personality test. Over the years, in various work and team settings, I have filled out questionnaires and been told what colour or number or series of letters I am. Whether it is the Enneagram, Myers Briggs or the Insights tests, I come out as quite an extreme extrovert. I get my energy from being around people. Nevertheless, increasingly as I have grown older, I have valued the moments of solitude and peace – especially after a busy period.

In the classic book *Men Are from Mars, Women Are from Venus*, written by John Gray in 1992, he describes how men like to retreat to their 'caves' during periods of stress, while women like to talk. This is perhaps an over-simplification, but in today's passage Luke tells us that Jesus would often withdraw to be alone – not simply to get away from people (although that might perhaps have been part of it) but to spend time with God, to pray to his heavenly Father.

This is an example to us all – whether we are extroverts or introverts. If Jesus needed to withdraw to lonely places and pray, then how much more should we? Life can get busy and overwhelming, with many demands and pressures on us, so many people to see and so much to do. When our to-do lists overflow, it can be tempting to spend all our time striving towards ticking things off, rather than spending time with God. Perhaps we might take our cue from Jesus, but also be reminded of the famous quote attributed to Martin Luther: 'I have so much to do that I shall spend the first three hours in prayer.'

God, in the busyness of our lives today, may we carve out time to be with you and be renewed by your Holy Spirit. Amen.

CHINE MCDONALD

THURSDAY 26 JUNE   **GALATIANS 5:13–26**

Fruit of the Spirit

But the fruit of the Spirit is love, joy, peace, forbearance, kindness, goodness, faithfulness, gentleness and self-control. Against such things there is no law. (vv. 22–23, NIV)

When I think about men as a collective, I am drawn towards characteristics that are generally ascribed to men, words like: strong, confident, logical, mechanically minded, rational, inexpressive (except when watching sport!) and so on. It is easy to stereotype whole groups of people. However, when I think about the individual men I know, I realise that men come in all varieties of characters and temperaments, with different strengths and qualities. Each one loved and made in the image of God.

    This passage reminds me that there are certain characteristics which should be modelled by both men and women as we grow in our relationship with Jesus. Being a Christian makes a difference to every part of our identity. Our motivations, behaviour and the way we treat others are changed day by day as the Holy Spirit guides us and works within us to change us into Christ's likeness.

    We are not called to live up to the world's patterns for how we should live as men and women; we are called to serve one another in love.

    Spend a few moments thinking about the men closest to you: your father, husband, brother, son, nephew or those who have previously played a significant part in your life. What fruit of the Spirt can you or did you see in their lives? Give thanks for the gifts God has given/gave them and pray that they will know God's leading and will grow into the men God has called them to be.

Holy God, thank you that you have made us in your image. Thank you for your grace in our lives and for your Holy Spirit. Help us to walk in the light of your love. Amen.

CHINE MCDONALD

FRIDAY 27 JUNE   **MARK 10:35–45**

To become great

Whoever wants to become great among you must be your servant, and whoever wants to be first must be slave of all. For even the Son of Man did not come to be served, but to serve, and to give his life as a ransom for many. (vv. 43–45, NIV)

James and John, described as the sons of Zebedee, are pretty bold in their request to Jesus. The gospels show that they and their fellow disciples treated Jesus with reverence, doing what he said, following where he led and calling him 'Rabbi', which meant teacher or master. Yet they clearly saw him as approachable enough for them to ask a very forthright question about their status in the kingdom of God.

In the preceding passage, Jesus tells his disciples what is going to happen to him: that he will be arrested, condemned to death, mocked, spat on, flogged and killed. It is not the first time that he has tried to explain this to them. The juxtaposition with James and John's request to Jesus therefore makes it all the more stark. They are following a leader who knows he is going to be subject to humiliation, but they are requesting to have the best seats – the most prominent seats – alongside Jesus in his glory.

Jesus tells them they don't know what they are asking. He explains to them that his kingdom is of another kind: that leadership looks very different there. It's about humility, serving others, laying down your life for people who follow you. I'm often reminded of the title of the book by Simon Sinek: *Leaders Eat Last*.

Jesus' model of male leadership is very different to what we see generally in the world and very often in our churches. Leadership today far too often prizes physical strength, toughness and other things that the world would describe as 'greatness'. What difference would it make to our world if our leaders sought to serve rather than be served?

Jesus, our servant king, we pray for all those in authority: strengthen their hearts and renew their minds. Help them to see the beauty of servant leadership. Amen.

CHINE MCDONALD

SATURDAY 28 JUNE   **LUKE 22:39–46**

Your will be done

He withdrew about a stone's throw beyond them, knelt down and prayed, 'Father, if you are willing, take this cup from me; yet not my will, but yours be done.' (vv. 41–42, NIV)

I never want anyone to tell my sons to 'man up'. This phrase – which has been ubiquitous in British culture since my childhood – is used to persuade men to be brave, to show courage, to do hard, manly things; to not show weakness. Not only does it imply that women are not those things, but it is also damaging to men. It encourages them to not reveal their vulnerabilities – even to themselves. It implies that men should have an unwavering strength, even when they are facing great difficulties and challenges.

Here, in the garden of Gethsemane, Jesus is facing the end of his life. Not only that, but he sits with the knowledge that he will shortly experience betrayal, isolation, unimaginable horror, violence and brutality. He knows he will go through this in front of crowds of people who will mock him. As if that were not enough, he will also take on the sins of the world upon himself and feel separate from God in a way that he will never have experienced. In a matter of hours, he will cry out, asking God why he has been forsaken.

Jesus is God in human flesh, yet Luke does not feel the need to hide away this story that shows Christ's vulnerability, as he asks God whether the cup can be taken from him. What might this teach a world that tells men to 'man up'? If Jesus can show his fear and anxiety, then surely we should encourage men to do the same without fear of judgement, and reassure them that they can bring their whole selves – vulnerabilities and all – to a God who loves them.

Loving God, when we feel overwhelmed and crippled with fear, help us to cast our burdens onto you. Amen.

CHINE MCDONALD

Learning from the life of Ruth

Rosemary Green writes…

I have found writing this series of notes on Ruth a challenge! I confess that I am less excited by this book than many Bible readers are. This has meant that it has been a good discipline for me to soak myself in its pages. It is too easy for us to read and reread our favourite parts of the Bible and to ignore the passages that attract us less or we find hard to understand.

I was asked to focus on Ruth herself, as last time this book was read in *Day by Day with God* the emphasis was on Naomi; but I find Ruth's character demonstrated in her interactions with the other main individuals in the story – Naomi and Boaz. Overall, I found the book of Ruth to be full of surprises, with customs and priorities very different from ours today.

The first and biggest surprise is that Ruth came from a nation, the Moabites, who had refused to help the Israelites on their long journey from Egypt to the promised land and later had hired Balaam to curse Israel. So the Moabites were anathema to the Jews; they did not allow any descendant of a Moabite to join Israel, down to the tenth generation (Deuteronomy 23:3–6). The prohibition against intermarriage was largely to preserve the Jews commitment to their one God; marriage with other nations too easily led to worship of other gods. This highlights the importance of Ruth's commitment in 1:16: 'Your people will be my people and your God my God' (NIV). It appears that one main purpose of the book was to validate the inclusion of Ruth as King David's great-grandmother.

The second big thing I had to grapple with was understanding the principle of the guardian-redeemer and then what looked at first sight like the apparent impropriety of Ruth throwing herself at Boaz, going to lie at his feet in the night when he was asleep on the threshing floor, where no woman was expected to be present. It seemed very strange, yet it was all part of the working out of God's purposes for the nation. God's name is only mentioned twice in the book, yet there is a sense of his hand in control behind the scenes.

I hope you will enjoy learning from this surprising story.

SUNDAY 29 JUNE   RUTH 1:1–5

The scene is set

In the days when the judges ruled, there was a famine in the land. So a man from Bethlehem in Judah, together with his wife and two sons, went to live for a while in the country of Moab. (v. 1, NIV)

The opening words of this book are ominous. Twice in the book of Judges we read, 'In those days Israel had no king; everyone did as they saw fit' (17:6, 21:25). So Elimelek, with his wife Naomi and their sons, weren't too bothered when they deliberately broke the rules that had been clearly laid down – no consorting with the Moabites, and that meant no intermarriage (Deuteronomy 23:3–6). Perhaps they reasoned, 'After all, Lord, there is a famine in the land. And we are not going forever.' It is easy to start making excuses to the Lord for our disobedience.

I learnt a very painful lesson, some 40 years ago, of the folly of disobedience or procrastination. God made it clear to me in June that a particular friendship was too important in my life and needed to change. 'Yes, Lord, I will – in September when things start afresh.' But between June and September the friendship crashed, disastrously. I learnt my lesson. Obedience to God matters.

Worse was to come for Elimelek's family. Within ten years, Elimelek died; the boys grew up and both married Moabite women, Orpah and Ruth. But the young men, too, died, without children. The three women were left on their own, without male protection. They must have felt helpless, and in a real dilemma.

This became God's opportunity to turn the situation around. Our God is a surprising God. He expects us to obey his rules. Yet he, the righteous God who makes no mistakes, can incorporate even our disobedience into working out his divine plans.

When you are feeling low and discouraged, can you turn to God in confidence that he does forgive our disobedience and that he will pick us up and lead us forward?

ROSEMARY GREEN

MONDAY 30 JUNE · **RUTH 1:6–22**

Leaving home

Ruth replied, 'Don't urge me to leave you or to turn back from you. Where you go I will go, and where you stay I will stay. Your people will be my people and your God my God. Where you die I will die, and there I will be buried.' (vv. 16–17, NIV)

After ten years in Moab, Naomi heard that there was food again in Israel, a sign that God was blessing his people; so the three women set out to return to Bethlehem. However, at Naomi's strong urging, Orpah decided to stay with her family, but Ruth was adamant that she would stick with her mother-in-law. This shows remarkable devotion in Ruth.

We do not know how much the older woman had talked about her people, her country, her lifestyle, her faith, or about the unwelcome reception the Moabitess might receive, but Ruth was willing to go into the unknown and commit herself to a new way of life with strangers in a new culture and with a new faith. This was not just temporarily, as when Elimelek and family went to Moab (v. 1) but for life (v. 17). What's more, Naomi herself recognised that she had become bitter through her bereavements; she no longer wanted to be called Naomi (meaning pleasant) but instead to be called Mara (meaning bitter). What sort of companion might she be for Ruth?

In a few short sentences we learn about Ruth's qualities of character. We see her initiative and her determination to step into the unknown. We see her willingness to adapt to new situations, new conditions and a new lifestyle. She demonstrates faith that was willing to cope with uncertainty and a commitment to stick for the rest of her life to all that was new and unfamiliar. Above all, she demonstrates her faithfulness to a mother-in-law who had lost her joy in life. The writer is setting out the case for Ruth being worthy to be part of the genealogy of the future king, despite her nationality.

Let's ask ourselves honestly how we compare with the qualities Ruth displayed. Then pray that the Holy Spirit may cultivate in us the characteristics where we see we fall short.

ROSEMARY GREEN

TUESDAY 1 JULY **RUTH 2:1–13**

Ruth meets Boaz

Boaz replied, 'I've been told all about what you have done for your mother-in-law since the death of your husband – how you left your father and mother and your homeland and came to live with a people you did not know before.' (v. 11, NIV)

God's generosity compels similar generosity from his people. When the farmers were harvesting, they would leave some stalks of grain lying loose so those without their own land could collect food. Ruth wanted to do what she could for her mother-in-law, so she suggested that she might go to glean with the other women. We don't know whether it was by her planning or by apparent chance that Ruth went to glean in fields belonging to Boaz, Elimelek's relative. Boaz didn't recognise this young woman among the regular gleaners, but word got round; he had heard the good reputation of the young Moabitess who had returned with Naomi. He told her to keep gleaning and to drink from the water jars when she was thirsty, and he told the young male harvesters not to molest her.

Although God's name is mentioned only twice in the book, there are ways in which we can sense his hand in guiding events. I wonder how often we stop to recognise God at work in unseen ways in our lives and in the lives of those around us. Can you look back over the past week and see ways God has been at work in your life? I know that when I strive too hard to make events in my diary fit, life can be tense and rushed. When I do more praying and less planning, I can see him bringing people along unexpectedly, either for me to serve them or for me to be helped.

Everything seems to be going well for Ruth. Remember the purpose behind the book, to commend Ruth as worthy to be an ancestor of King David, despite being from Moab.

A church often has an effective bush telegraph. Let's make sure that each one of us spreads news only to build others up, not to undermine reputations by false gossip.

ROSEMARY GREEN

WEDNESDAY 2 JULY   **RUTH 2:14–23**

Two-way generosity

Ruth gleaned in the field until evening. Then she threshed the barley she had gathered, and it amounted to about an ephah. She carried it back to town, and her mother-in-law saw how much she had gathered. (vv. 17–18, NIV)

There are several lovely marks of generosity in these verses. Boaz goes out of his way to show care for the stranger – for example, roasted grain for Ruth to eat and orders for stalks to be specially pulled out for her. Ruth too shows her generosity to Naomi in her hard work. Having laboured until the day's harvesting was finished, she stayed to thresh the barley she was going to take home. She had a bulky, heavy sack to carry; an ephah of barley, about 35 litres, weighed about 13 kg. She even remembered the spare roasted grain she had put aside at lunch to take to Naomi. And we see Naomi's bitterness being replaced by thankfulness as she recognised the ways both God and other people were caring for them.

I sometimes regret that Luke slipped into Acts one of Jesus' comments that doesn't appear in any of the gospels: 'It is more blessed to give than to receive' (Acts 20:35). When my husband was stuck in South Africa with meningitis, some 50 years ago, recovering more slowly than expected, I learnt that there is also a blessedness in receiving. There was a ring of friends around me saying in effect, 'Rosemary, please let us help you; please let us love you'. My initial response was to say stiffly, 'I'm all right. I can cope.' It was only when I let down my barriers of pride and independence that God was able to bless me with his love and to change me.

Some of us find it easier to give than to learn to receive – graciously, in helplessness – the generosity of others. I hope we can learn to be generous in our giving and gracious in our receiving.

Do you need to learn to be a generous giver or a gracious receiver – or both? I was deeply blessed when I learnt to receive.

ROSEMARY GREEN

THURSDAY 3 JULY RUTH 3:1–6

Important preparations

'My daughter, I must find a home for you, where you will be well provided for. Now Boaz, with whose women you have worked, is a relative of ours. Tonight he will be winnowing barley on the threshing-floor. Wash, put on perfume, and get dressed in your best clothes.'
(vv. 1–3, NIV)

Naomi had already told Ruth that Boaz was not just a close relative but that he was also a guardian-redeemer – a close male relative who ensured that the inheritance of both estate and family name would not be lost by buying the property and marrying the widow. This is a strange concept to us, but normal in that culture. (We read of a similar situation in the gospels, in Matthew 22:23–28, when the Sadducees came to Jesus with a trick question about a woman who had been passed as a bride from one dying brother to another.)

It was nearing the end of harvest-time, and Naomi was probably anxious to see Ruth settled before Boaz returned to his home. I wonder if Ruth was surprised at her mother-in-law's instructions! Nevertheless, she did all that Naomi told her to do.

Ruth must have experienced considerable culture shock when she went to live in Bethlehem, among new people and new customs, but she had made a promise to Naomi: 'Your people will be my people.' If she felt any homesickness for her family and the home of her birth, she did not show it. Her commitment to Naomi was wholehearted.

Ruth doesn't appear to have any regrets. Do you ever look back on your life and wish that you had made some different decisions? Living with regrets can sap our energy and our joy. We cannot change past events, but we can ask God to change the effects those events still have on us. I'm not saying it's easy, but God's forgiveness and his power are huge; he can help us to commit ourselves to looking forward, not backwards, so that the 'if onlys' of our regrets no longer need to drag us down.

Pray for yourself Paul's prayer in Ephesians 1:19–20. May I know 'his incomparably great power for us who believe. That power is the same as the mighty strength he exerted when he raised Christ from the dead.' Wow!

ROSEMARY GREEN

FRIDAY 4 JULY RUTH 3:7–18

A bold move

[Boaz replied] 'This kindness is greater than that which you showed earlier: you have not run after the younger men, whether rich or poor. And now, my daughter, don't be afraid. I will do for you all you ask. All the people of my town know that you are a woman of noble character.' (vv. 10–11, NIV)

At first sight our reaction to Ruth's behaviour might be 'shameless hussy!' as she appears to throw herself at Boaz. It seems a risky move, to go so close to a sleeping man after his late-night partying. However, she was following her mother-in-law's instructions, she understood the cultural expectation of the guardian-redeemer, and she had seen enough of Boaz to respect him and to trust him. It appears a strange way of going about things, but she was inviting him to fulfil his responsibilities, privately in darkness rather than publicly in daylight. He, in return, respected all that he had heard and seen of Ruth and her character, and he wanted to do right by her. He protected her reputation, sending her home before daylight; he gave her a generous provision of grain and he promised to contact the relation who was an even closer guardian-redeemer.

I doubt if Naomi had much sleep that night, as she wondered how things were going for her daughter-in-law and waited for her return! She was fully content to hear Ruth's account of the night's events and had no doubt that Boaz would act quickly and honourably.

All worked out well in this particular situation, but I would not want to commend Ruth's behaviour as an example for any young woman to follow. There was plenty of sexual aberration in Bible times and there is certainly plenty today. We want to do all in our power to ensure that we are squeaky clean in our own sexual behaviour, and in the example and guidance we give to other – especially younger – women towards whom we have responsibility.

Lord, please bring me up short if there is any way in which I have displeased you in my own sexual behaviour. Thank you that you forgive and cleanse. And show me how best to help others stay pure. Amen.

ROSEMARY GREEN

SATURDAY 5 JULY — **RUTH 4**

Inheritance assured

So Boaz took Ruth and she became his wife. When he made love to her, the Lord enabled her to conceive, and she gave birth to a son… And they named him Obed. He was the father of Jesse, the father of David. (vv. 13, 17, NIV)

Naomi was right. Boaz wasted no time in approaching the (unnamed) relation to ask if he wanted to redeem both Elimelek's property and his daughter-in-law. The man was eager to own more land, but he balked at the thought of a wife! Boaz had already gathered ten of the town's elders to witness any transaction. In lieu of signing a document, the man threw down his sandal, in the presence of many witnesses, to confirm his withdrawal from the deal. The way was clear for Boaz to marry Ruth, who bore him a son, Obed. But Granny Naomi was allowed to do much of the babycare! That shows graciousness in Ruth, willing to hand over much of the care of a baby for whom she had been waiting for some years, since she had married Naomi's son Kilion (Ruth 1:4–5).

We might see this book as primarily a love story between Ruth and Boaz; or as the demonstration of a faithful daughter-in-law; or as the way God (though rarely mentioned) worked out his purposes. I see the main aim as being to establish King David's ancestry. The writer of the book has done enough to establish Ruth's character; he has shown her as an exemplary woman, faithful to mother-in-law Naomi, bearing a son in the line of succession, worthy (despite being from Moab) to be an ancestor of the future King David. The Jews laid much store by their genealogies, so as well as looking forward to David, the writer traces the line back to Judah, fourth son of Isaac's wife Leah. (This includes some dubious events in the birth of Boaz's ancestor Perez; you could read Genesis 38 if you like.)

We can see God working out his purposes in this story. Look back at your own life, and thank God for ways you can see, in retrospect, his hand on you even if you were unaware of it at the time.

ROSEMARY GREEN

Making all things new: God's justice

Hannah Fytche writes…

One of my favourite books is C.S. Lewis' *The Lion, the Witch and the Wardrobe*. It's a story of a cold winter and a long-awaited spring. The inhabitants of Narnia wait and work for a new day when the dominion of the White Witch is overthrown and Aslan sets all things right and makes all things new.

This hope is captured in words with which the Narnians continually reassure each other – words of wrongs being made right and spring coming forth from winter when Aslan arrives. You can see C.S. Lewis drawing on the Christian tradition in the words of hope he places in the Narnian voices. Aslan is the Christ-figure whose coming – and eventual death and resurrection – brings healing to the world. In his presence, sorrow melts. By his power, injustice and oppression are broken. Through his life, spring arrives.

This kind of justice, the righting of wrongs and the restoration of all things, is what we will explore through the next two weeks. We'll start with Jesus' proclamation of how he will bring God's promised renewal. We'll consider how people react to this announcement, recognising that Jesus' justice potentially disrupts old ways of life in order to bring new restoration. Stories of Jesus' teaching and enacting justice through his life, death and resurrection will help us to explore this tension between disruption and restoration in the pursuit of justice.

During the second week, we'll turn to three songs of justice, sung by Mary, Hannah, and Miriam and Moses. These songs are examples of people's responses to God's justice enacted in particular circumstances, and they will inspire us to think about how we seek and respond to God's justice in our own lives. Our final three days will prompt us to consider how we can put all we've discovered into practice.

With this in mind, let's begin with a prayer.

Christ Jesus, you make all things new. Open my eyes and heart to your radical justice over the next two weeks, and lead me to join with you in your work of transforming the world through your death and resurrection. May you show me where in my own life I can partner with you to contribute to a more just world. Amen.

SUNDAY 6 JULY — **LUKE 4:14–21**

Jesus proclaims justice

'The Spirit of the Lord is on me, because he has anointed me to proclaim good news to the poor. He has sent me to proclaim freedom for the prisoners and recovery of sight for the blind, to set the oppressed free, to proclaim the year of the Lord's favour.' (vv. 18–19, NIV)

As Luke's gospel tells the story, Jesus emerges from 40 days of wilderness trials and, in the power of the Spirit, returns to his hometown. In the synagogue, he announces to those gathered that he is the one anointed by God's Spirit, the one of whom scripture speaks. He fulfils the prophecy that he reads from Isaiah.

Isaiah's words prophesy justice, good news for the poor, freedom for prisoners, sight for those who are blind, an end to oppression, the Lord's favour: these are all glimmers of a world made right. Isaiah imagines a world made new, and Jesus says he's here to make that vision a reality.

I would have loved to have been there when Jesus claimed these words for himself. In my imagination everything quietens and stills as Jesus looks up from the scroll from which he's reading. The congregation hold their breath. Even the air seems to hold its breath – the atmosphere is electric, expectant, as Jesus speaks those words that seem to say 'Here I am! A world made whole and right is coming through me; I am making all things new. Freedom and healing are on their way.'

It's as if the whole world has been waiting – aching! – to hear this beautiful proclamation of restoration.

I suspect we all ache for such promises to be made true, repairing all that's hurt or broken. We don't have to search far to find injustice: our world is full of it. Listen to the news and you'll find dozens of headlines which proclaim the world's heartbreak. I imagine you may have experienced different forms of injustice, too. Feel the ache of it. Then imagine yourself hearing Jesus say he's here to bring relief from the pain. Here he is, proclaiming God's justice. Restoration is on its way.

Consider how God's 'justice' that Jesus brings in vv. 18–19 is described. Which one resonates most? What other words might you use to describe 'justice'?

HANNAH FYTCHE

MONDAY 7 JULY   **LUKE 4:22–30**

A disruptive justice

All the people in the synagogue were furious when they heard this. They got up, drove him out of the town, and took him to the brow of the hill on which the town was built, in order to throw him off the cliff. But he walked right through the crowd and went on his way.
(vv. 28–30, NIV)

After Jesus' proclamation of God's justice, a dispute breaks out. His listeners doubt the veracity of Jesus' claim: surely *Jesus*, Joseph's son, can't be the one promised by God to bring this to life!

Jesus responds with stories in which those who are not God's people receive God's blessing through Elijah, while God's people reject him. He says a prophet is rarely received as such by their own people, but the truth of their prophetic claims is not undermined. Though Jesus' listeners doubt him, what he says is true.

Angered further, Jesus' listeners drive him out of town. I wonder what was so offensive about Jesus' claims. Was it something to do with what will be required to bring God's justice to life?

Jesus speaks of justice for those who are on the margins of society: the poor, the prisoners, the oppressed and those from outside of the community of God's people. This is disruptive. To bring restoration to marginalised people requires an upending of societal norms. For the powerful, it means recognising complicity in the act of marginalising others; and for all of us, it requires inclusion of those who hadn't before been included.

As an example, we could think about our supply chains – the global systems that bring food to our plates and clothes to our bodies. Much within these systems is unjust. To bring restoration to those harmed by them would require a disruption of the ways in which we have come to live. It would require an overhaul of economic and social patterns, and while we can all agree this is just, it is also disruptive.

While his listeners are engrossed in their arguments, Jesus goes on his way, journeying to restore all things through his life, death and resurrection.

God's justice calls for restoration of the marginalised and othered. Who are those people in our world today? How can we find healing together (especially when this disrupts our own patterns of living)?

HANNAH FYTCHE

TUESDAY 8 JULY   **LUKE 10:25–37**

The parable of the good Samaritan

He answered, 'Love the Lord your God with all your heart and with all your soul and with all your strength and with all your mind'; and, 'Love your neighbour as yourself.' (v. 27, NIV)

'Who is my neighbour?', the lawyer asks. Jesus tells the parable of the good Samaritan to reimagine what it means to 'love your neighbour'. Today, being a Samaritan stands for being compassionate and caring for those who are in need. We are put in the Samaritan's shoes and told to emulate his actions. *We* are the ones who help *others*, even if they are our enemy or different than us. We are not the ones in need.

Might there be another perspective from which we could view this parable? Parables have multiple meanings: instead of imagining ourselves as the Samaritan, we could imagine ourselves as the man left for dead.

Then we might ask, 'Who will help me?' Contrary to expectation, the Levite and priest, afraid of stopping on this dangerous road, don't help.

The Samaritan, the enemy, helps. To Jesus' Jewish audience this would've been shocking. It perhaps even evoked a response of 'I'd rather be left for dead than be helped by a *Samaritan*.' The enmity between the people groups was this visceral. The neighbour in Jesus' parable cannot be a Samaritan! (Read more about this in Amy-Jill Levine's *Short Stories by Jesus*.)

Yet if this meaning of 'neighbour' is refused, then the man in the parable is left for dead. To refuse the Samaritan as a neighbour is to refuse the help he offers. This is where we find our reflection on justice. God's justice doesn't always look like *us* helping *others*, but also us recognising that we *are* the others, needing to receive help from those we might view as the enemy. Justice comes through our humility to see God's new life at work for us through those we might not expect – even if that totally disrupts our previous perspectives.

Who are 'enemies' in your life – or the ones from whom you wouldn't normally accept help? How might you learn to see them anew as your neighbour, one through whom new life and hope can come into your life?

HANNAH FYTCHE

WEDNESDAY 9 JULY   **LUKE 11:1–13**

Praying for God's justice

'Father, hallowed be your name, your kingdom come. Give us each day our daily bread. Forgive us our sins, for we also forgive everyone who sins against us. And lead us not into temptation.' (vv. 2–4, NIV)

'Pray the Lord's Prayer twice a day, and let it reveal to you who God is with you and in this world.' This is a paraphrase of some advice a friend once gave to someone curious about the Christian faith. Pray the words Jesus taught twice a day and let them inform your imagination of what God is like and how God acts in the world. Let them show you a vision of what God's goodness and justice can look like in our lives.

God's justice looks like needs met: daily bread in the hands of each hungry person. It looks like forgiveness: relationships repaired even when they've been broken. It looks like a way through temptation: a way we can walk that leads to life rather than destruction.

God's justice looks like the kingdom being made present among us in all these ways.

Jesus teaches us to pray for such restorative justice – pray his words twice a day; pray them more! May they inform your imagination of God bringing life that you can join in with making a reality.

May you be reassured, too, that it will become a reality, even against the odds of this unjust world. After teaching his disciples this prayer, Jesus continues his teaching, saying: 'Ask and it will be given to you.' God is even more loving than the most loving parent: through prayer, God offers abundant gifts to his children.

When we pray with this vision of a world brought to life by God's love, our imaginations become shaped by it. We begin to see the world as God sees it – and when we see with this vision, we come to live in such a way that makes that vision more of a reality. Father, your kingdom come.

How might you allow this prayer to inform your imagination of the just world God is bringing? Which words capture your imagination, and how might they reveal where God is bringing restoration in your life and the lives of others?

HANNAH FYTCHE

THURSDAY 10 JULY   **LUKE 13:10–17**

Jesus enacts justice: on the sabbath

When Jesus saw her, he called her forward and said to her, 'Woman, you are set free from your infirmity.' Then he put his hands on her, and immediately she straightened up and praised God. (v. 12, NIV)

Jesus lives and breathes God's justice. Today's reading, as well as those for the next few days, are gospel stories which illuminate how Jesus brings healing through his life, death and resurrection.

In today's story, Jesus pauses his teaching in a synagogue as he sees a woman 'crippled by a spirit for eighteen years. She was bent over and could not straighten up' (v. 11). This woman lives with chronic illness ('spirits' are often best understood in the New Testament as being to do with conditions which we know today are caused by mental or physical illness, injury or sickness). Her chronic illness has her bent over in pain. Her life will have been severely limited. Jesus pauses in his teaching to heal her.

This is a very personal instance of restoration. It shows us that, at its heart, God's justice is about compassion for people. God cares for each one of us, for the particular burdens we bear and the specific scars we carry. Jesus makes all people, each one of us, new.

As well as revealing the deeply personal nature of God's justice, this is also a story (once again) of the disruptive nature of justice. Jesus heals this woman on the sabbath – the day on which no work should be done. This angers the synagogue leader, and Jesus responds by helping his listeners to reimagine the ways in which God works. Why shouldn't the woman be set free on the sabbath?

Jesus disrupts expectations of how God brings restoration. He brings new life to old patterns of living – old ways of following God. He doesn't discard these old ways, but instead reimagines them. Disruptive and personal: God's justice is both wonderfully restorative and potentially uncomfortable. Jesus is doing a new thing. May we perceive it.

Jesus, may compassion disrupt my expectations of your justice. As I seek to live justly, may I prioritise those you love rather than my own preconceptions about how to love them. Amen.

HANNAH FYTCHE

FRIDAY 11 JULY LUKE 8:40–48

Jesus enacts justice: for the outcasts

And a woman was there who had been subject to bleeding for twelve years, but no one could heal her. She came up behind him and touched the edge of his cloak, and immediately her bleeding stopped.
(vv. 43–44, NIV)

Today's story is another in which we see Jesus enacting personal justice. A woman has been bleeding for twelve years. She's risking much by coming to Jesus because according to her culture's customs, her ailment means that she shouldn't be seen, heard or touched.

This woman is marginalised by the expectations of her world. Yet she does an extraordinary thing and reaches for healing from the hem of Jesus' cloak – sneaking a touch which, by her faith, heals her. Jesus responds to this brave act with welcome. The woman is seen, known and loved. She is moved from the margins to the centre of Jesus' attention.

When I think about injustice, the word 'marginalised' springs to mind. Those whom injustice deeply affects are often those discriminated against or pushed to the edges of communities by those at the powerful centre. We see this dynamic at work in many contexts. Systemic racism and sexism marginalise people on the basis of race and gender, respectively. A class system marginalises people on the basis of wealth and sometimes geography. Many of us are victims of such injustices as these. This is painful – and I pray that when experiencing such pain we find in Christ someone who sees, knows and loves us.

Yet many of us are also complicit in such injustices, caught up in the expectations of our cultures. The work of justice is to repent of this complicity and to rise from the place of repentance with humility that helps us to be like Christ in seeing and knowing each person as loved and worthy. In Christ, there is always enough space at the centre: no one need be marginalised. A world restored is one in which we all find seats at the feast, welcomed there by Christ and each other.

Jesus, you see and know me. Show me where I have not lived up to your compassion by marginalising others. Create in my communities relationships in which I am seen and known and in which I see and know others. Amen.

HANNAH FYTCHE

SATURDAY 12 JULY   **JOHN 13:1–17**

Justice through humility

Jesus knew that the Father had put all things under his power, and that he had come from God and was returning to God; so he got up from the meal, took off his outer clothing, and wrapped a towel round his waist. (vv. 3–4, NIV)

We have been reading about Jesus proclaiming, teaching and enacting the restorative justice that he'll bring through his life, death and resurrection, and we've considered how this kind of justice can disrupt and upset our expectations, perspectives and social systems.

This combination of restoration and disruption is seen again in this intimate story, in which Jesus, just before he died, kneels to wash his friends' feet. Aware of the power with which God anoints him, Jesus upends expectations of how God's anointed should bring justice. People expected God to send a saviour who was mighty in power – not one who knelt with a towel around his waist. Yet Christ brings new life through becoming a servant.

Simon Peter voices his confusion, his ideas about Jesus disrupted: 'Lord, are you going to wash my feet?' *Surely not*. Jesus points towards his death and resurrection as he replies: 'You do not realise now what I am doing, but later you will understand' (vv. 6–7).

After Jesus' resurrection his friends will understand that Jesus' justice does not come through a mighty battle, but through Jesus humbling himself to the death of the cross. Restoration comes by having our feet washed by Christ – by finding ourselves made whole and holy through Jesus' death and brought to life through his resurrection.

This, I think, is the most astonishing disruption of all. Christ's death disrupts every hierarchy of power; no one was expecting God's salvation of the world to come through a crucifixion. Yet as Christ's body is broken so too is every system of oppression and injustice which holds people captive rather than liberates them. As Christ's body is raised, death in all its guises is overcome. Amen and amen.

Dwell with the image of Christ kneeling to wash our feet, defeating injustice in our lives and our world through humility and service. Imagine yourself into the scene. What do you say to Jesus? What does he say to you?

HANNAH FYTCHE

SUNDAY 13 JULY
ROMANS 5:1–11

Christ's reconciling justice

You see, at just the right time, when we were still powerless, Christ died for the ungodly. Very rarely will anyone die for a righteous person, though for a good person someone might possibly dare to die. But God demonstrates his own love for us in this. (vv. 6–8, NIV)

These words are written by Paul, one of the first missionaries proclaiming the gospel of Jesus Christ's death and resurrection. Paul writes these words to the first Christian communities in Rome, and through the letter to the Romans, you can see him working out what it means for people's lives to be transformed and restored through this gospel.

It's a big question: what *does* it mean to find our lives in Christ's new life? What does justice look like in light of Jesus' life, death and resurrection? In Paul's words: we have peace (v. 1); we have access to God's grace and hope in his glory (v. 2); we have hope even in the midst of suffering, because right there with us is the Holy Spirit poured into our hearts (v. 5); we are reconciled to God (vv. 10–11).

Peace, grace, hope and the presence of God with us – for each of us as individuals, and as communities, this is the justice we receive through Christ. I love the word 'reconciled' as a description of this restoration: we are reconciled, made whole and complete, through our friendship with God in Christ. It is a vision of new life which makes me feel totally at peace, held safe in the power and love of Christ.

As well as providing peace, this sense of justice as reconciliation brings a challenge. Which relationships with friends, colleagues or neighbours need reconciliation? Against whom do I complain or grumble? Who do I exclude, ignore or distance myself from? Living my life in Christ means answering these questions by pursuing reconciliation even in difficult relationships – even when it disrupts my own sense of pride or patterns of relating to others.

We find friendship in you, Jesus – friendship which reconciles us to God and to each other. May this vision of your reconciling justice be realised in my own relationships. Amen.

HANNAH FYTCHE

MONDAY 14 JULY LUKE 1:46–55

Songs of justice: Mary

'He has brought down rulers from their thrones but has lifted up the humble. He has filled the hungry with good things but has sent the rich away empty.' (vv. 52–53, NIV)

Today we encounter our first of three songs which paint rich and powerful pictures of God's justice. Each song arises from a personal situation in which God has acted: the singers are reflecting on what has happened in their lives by exploring what it shows them about God.

This first song is from Mary, Jesus' mother. At this stage in Luke's gospel, Mary is pregnant with Jesus. She has gone to stay with her cousin Elizabeth, who is pregnant with John (who will baptise Jesus). Amidst the joy of their realisation that God is fulfilling his promises through their pregnancies (1:39–45), Mary sings this song of praise.

Through the song God's justice is revealed to be the kind of justice we've seen so many times in the past days: a justice that disrupts expectations and turns the patterns and hierarchies of our lives and our world on their head.

Proud, arrogant people are scattered: they tumble from the pedestals that they place themselves on. Humble people are lifted: those perceived as weak are treasured by God and given all that they need. The hungry are fed and the rich are hungry. Mary sings this song of God's justice, a song that will come to describe the restorative effects of Jesus' life, death and resurrection.

Mary's song is very familiar to me. Her words are part of Evening Prayer in my church tradition, which means that I've had seasons where I've prayed these words with people several times a week. With repetition, these words have come to shape my imagination of what God is doing in the world. They are becoming words that I want to sing with Mary – words that I want to see sung over our world until all is set right, God's justice restoring all that has been broken.

Are there texts from the Bible, songs that you sing, poems or pieces of artwork that are forming your imagination of what a just world could look like? What do they reveal to you about God and the restoration God is bringing?

HANNAH FYTCHE

TUESDAY 15 JULY **1 SAMUEL 2:1–10**

Songs of justice: Hannah

'He raises the poor from the dust and lifts the needy from the ash heap; he seats them with princes and makes them inherit a throne of honour.' (v. 8, NIV)

Here is our second song of justice: Hannah's song. Hannah was unable to have a child, and she prayed daily at the temple to become pregnant. Eventually she conceived and bore a son. These words are her song of praise in response, revealing who Hannah has experienced God to be.

I am not suggesting that God's justice for those who are childless always involves God making them able to have children. There can be deep pain and many unanswered prayers in childlessness, and God meeting someone in this pain looks different for different people.

For Hannah, the response she gives to the particular way God meets her in her pain is this song of praise. In her song she reflects, like Mary, on the ways in which God disrupts the hierarchies of the world in order to bring restoration. The poor are lifted up; those who have need are cared for and given an inheritance.

Do you notice the similarities between Hannah's and Mary's songs? Mary likely knew Hannah's song, and she claims some of those words and expressions of who God is for herself. This is incredible, I think. These two women, separated by millennia and in different circumstances, encounter the same God bringing the same disruptive, restorative justice. Who God is, God has always been and will always be.

We each live in different circumstances, and our lives are uniquely our own – yet we are bound by our common experience of a God who is making all things new. I love it when I find myself in conversations of sharing stories of God's goodness. Through very different stories and experiences, God is again and again revealed to be the same God who always tends towards new life.

Could you and your friends or community share ways in which God's justice and healing has been present in your lives? What similarities are there across your encounters of God, and what does this reveal about who God is?

HANNAH FYTCHE

WEDNESDAY 16 JULY EXODUS 15:1–21

Songs of justice: Miriam and Moses

Miriam sang to them: 'Sing to the Lord, for he is highly exalted. Both horse and driver he has hurled into the sea.' (v. 21, NIV)

In the movie *The Prince of Egypt*, there's a joyous scene after Moses leads God's people through the Red Sea to safety. Everyone sings a song of praise. Some children sing in Hebrew, the language of God's people: they are singing parts of the 'Song of the Sea', Miriam and Moses' song that we read today.

It's a song of victory, praise, joy and strength. God has rescued his people, and he has hurled their oppressors into the sea! The deep injustice endured by the Hebrew people has been overthrown. Let us similarly praise God for the overcoming of injustices through the death and resurrection of Christ and the freedom this has brought in our lives.

Yet let us als pause and consider a challenging question implicit in Moses and Miriam's song: is it really just and fair for God to hurl people into the sea, even if they are the oppressors? Is it right for God to favour some people and punish others?

I don't have answers to these questions – aside from recognising that justice is complex, layered with grey rather than clarified in black and white (as Moses and Miriam's song might make it seem). As we have considered (with the story of the bleeding woman, on 11 July), people can be both victims of injustice *and* complicit in the complex injustices of our world. It is hard to identify who in today's world God 'should' hurl into the sea: who exactly are the oppressors and who are the oppressed?

Again: no answers. I am drawn to a desire to trust justice to God's hands and to keep holding these hands so that I might learn from God about how to seek life even in complex questions of justice.

Jesus Christ, even as we praise you for the justice you bring, it reminds us of the complexity of justice. May you guide us, bringing us to repentance over our complicity and to new vision as we follow you. Amen.

HANNAH FYTCHE

THURSDAY 17 JULY   **ISAIAH 61**

An ancient call to justice

'The Spirit of the Sovereign Lord is on me, because the Lord has anointed me to proclaim good news to the poor. He has sent me to bind up the broken-hearted, to proclaim freedom for the captives and release from darkness for the prisoners, to proclaim the year of the Lord's favour…' (vv. 1–2a, NIV)

As we move towards the end of our series on God's justice, we return to familiar words. In Isaiah 61 we find the words that Jesus read and claimed in his hometown synagogue. Jesus' words are not new. They are ancient words of God's people, showing us that God's justice is long-lasting and deep-rooted. God has forever been known to be a just God, seeking restoration and healing for all that has been broken.

This continuity with ancient words reassures me: what God has always been, God will always be. Even when we are not sure how God's promises of restoration will come true, we can nevertheless trust that they will. What God has done, God can do again – always through Christ, who claims these ancient words anew and brings them to life through his death and resurrection.

Today I want to invite you to look back in your own life and notice where God's justice and restoration have been present. Are there moments in which you or those you know have experienced God's healing and new life? Can you think of times when you have seen justice enacted in your community, country or world? Are there organisations in your community which are working to bring restoration to lives that have been harmed?

As you notice these things, give thanks for them. Allow them to become the foundation of your trust in God for the days, weeks and years ahead. God has been just, and always will be – and will always be inspiring people to work for justice in our communities. Pray that God might inspire you and show you how you can build on those foundations of God's trustworthy character. How is God leading you to join in with bringing justice to those whom he loves?

Loving God, through Christ you anoint me with your Spirit: the same Spirit present in Isaiah's time and who sent Christ to bind up broken hearts. Show me how to partner with you in bringing justice. Amen.

HANNAH FYTCHE

FRIDAY 18 JULY MICAH 6:5–8

The continuing call to justice

He has shown you, O mortal, what is good. And what does the Lord require of you? To act justly and to love mercy and to walk humbly with your God. (v. 8, NIV)

We've spent nearly two weeks with visions of God's justice, discovering how God is making all things new. God has shown us what is good; may it continue to form our imaginations about a world restored.

As we continue to think about God's justice, how might we respond to it? Words from Micah, a prophetic book in the Old Testament, give us an idea: act justly, love mercy and walk humbly with God.

Together these instructions make me think of going on a long walk, concentrating on putting one foot in front of the other in pursuit of a beauti-ful destination. Acting justly, loving mercy, and walking humbly are not grand actions: they don't claim to dazzlingly fix all the world's injustices, and they don't call attention to themselves. Rather, in the midst of a world that endures so much brokenness and heartache, these actions are a way to keep walking well through it all. With each intentional step, taken with justice, mercy and humility, we contribute to the realisation of a more just world.

This weekend, notice how you can show justice, mercy, humility, kindness and love. How can you contribute to the restoration of the world in which you live? It might look like meeting the needs of someone you encounter, by providing them with friendship, food, material help or hope – or it might look like having *your* needs met by someone who cares for you. It might look like choosing where you buy from: buying food or clothes from ethical sources chips away at unjust systems in supply chains. It might look like joining in a conversation at your church about how you might become a more 'green' or 'eco-friendly' church – are there ways that you could together contribute to the restoration of our planet?

Almighty God, you call us to live in light of your heart for the restoration of all that you have made and all that you love. Direct my steps: show me how to contribute to making all things new. Amen.

HANNAH FYTCHE

SATURDAY 19 JULY — HABAKKUK 1:1–4, 3:17–18

When injustice is overwhelming

Though the fig-tree does not bud and there are no grapes on the vines … yet I will rejoice in the Lord, I will be joyful in God my Saviour. (vv. 17–18, NIV)

While we keep walking well through the world's injustice, seeking to bring healing and restoration with all that we do, it can be easy to become discouraged. There is so much that remains to be done in order for all things to be made new. How do we keep going when injustice threatens to overwhelm us?

The prophet Habakkuk wrestled with the same question. Fig trees and grapevines were fruitless. No blossoms appeared; grapes and figs didn't ripen. Crops failed. Livestock died. People grew hungry, starving. Communities and ways of living crumbled. Hope flickered and faded.

We can translate Habakkuk's words for our own context, recognising that both we and Habakkuk can look out at the world and see all the ways that it hurts. The planet is still warming, and efforts to slow the effects of climate change are seemingly fruitless. Violence and conflict continue in various parts of the world, tearing apart lives, families, and countries. Racism and misogyny are still prevalent in our cultures, curtailing lives. I could go on, and I'm sure you could add your own examples of injustice to the list. It can be overwhelming.

How do we keep going? We turn to our God and rejoice in the restoration we know that God will bring. We imagine ourselves back into that synagogue in Jesus' hometown and hear him claim those words from Isaiah for himself. We have faith that this claim is true as we repeatedly return to Jesus' death and resurrection: death in all its guises is overcome by Christ's new life and enlivened by his power and love.

In rejoicing so in Christ Jesus, we find our strength to keep going – to keep acting justly, loving mercy and walking humbly with our God, who will bring new life, finally, to it all.

Have you ever felt overwhelmed by injustice and heartbreak? Perhaps you could memorise Habakkuk's words as a way of praying for God to be with you and to guide you in pursuing new life.

HANNAH FYTCHE

How to make good decisions

Lyndall Bywater writes:

Are you a decisive person, or are you the sort of person who goes round and round the options for weeks before you settle on your final choice? I almost missed out on having a 50th birthday meal the other week because it took me so long to decide which restaurant I wanted to go to, so you can probably work out which camp I fall into!

For the next two weeks, we're going to be thinking about how to make good decisions, and we're going to explore what advice the Bible offers on the subject. Decisions come in all shapes and sizes, but the bigger ones can be daunting. Not being able to decide which restaurant to go to isn't really a serious problem, but when it comes to things like where you live, what job you do, what you do with your money or how you navigate a particularly difficult relationship, decision-making gets much more stressful. It's easy to get tangled up in indecision or to jump the gun and do something you end up regretting.

I have some pretty important decisions to make in my own life at the moment, and I asked God what I might do to help me in my decision-making process. The answer surprised me. God told me to gather lots of perfume samples and to try a different one each day during Lent. I wasn't quite sure what that had to do with the important decisions I needed to make, but I did it. Each day I sprayed a different fragrance. Most I liked, some I didn't, but each scent did its work. Some were exciting, new, invigorating, inspiring me for new possibilities and distant places, while others were familiar and warm, reminding me of people who love me.

The thing about perfume is that, once you've sprayed it, it sits there on your skin, enveloping you in fragrance and you don't have to do anything else to make it work. It was a reminder to me that I am held. Though none of those perfumes answered my big questions, the practice has left me steadier, calmer and more able to put my trust in God.

As you journey through these reflections with me, I pray you'll find things that help you, but most of all I pray you will know yourself enveloped in the love of God.

SUNDAY 20 JULY GENESIS 2:15—3:8

The companion

Then the man and his wife heard the sound of the Lord God as he was walking in the garden in the cool of the day, and they hid from the Lord God among the trees of the garden. (v. 8, NIV)

This morning, I mentioned to a friend that I was about to start writing Bible notes on how to make good decisions. Without missing a beat, she responded: 'I presume you're going to start by telling them about the importance of a good cup of tea!' I laughed, but I wonder if she might be on to something.

We begin our ponderings on how to make good decisions with the very first story told in the Bible. Adam and Eve have been given a beautiful place to live. But it's not just a beautiful place, it's a place with a presence. We learn from Genesis 3:8 that God is to be found there. God walks there, and since that particular verse tells us that Adam and Eve were hiding from God, we can assume that God walks there out of a desire to be with them.

Making good decisions can feel lonely. It can feel like we're trying to work out what to do, while a stern, mysterious God watches us to see if we get it right. Yet nothing could be further from the truth. Ours is a God who loves to walk and talk with us, to keep us company as we tackle life's decisions.

The decision-making in Eden starts early, since Adam gets to name his fellow creatures. I love imagining those animal-naming conversations: God and Adam talking together about what to call the creature with the long neck, or the one with humps on its back. In my mind's eye, it's always a convrsation full of fun, completely at ease, one that might even involve a good cup of tea. If a cup of tea (or other beverage) helps you remember that God loves to keep you company in your decision-making, then it really is a great place to start.

Next time you sit down to ponder a decision, have a cup of your favourite comforting beverage to hand as a reminder that you are not alone and that God wants to give you peace in your decision-making.

LYNDALL BYWATER

MONDAY 21 JULY   **JOHN 14:1–14**

The road

'I am the Road, also the Truth, also the Life. No one gets to the Father apart from me.' (v. 6, MSG)

I was reading an article recently about how 'smart roads' will be arriving in the next couple of decades. At the moment, a road is essentially a stretch of land specially hardened and marked out for us to travel along, but in years to come, roads will become high-tech. Thanks to various different technologies, they will feed us information about the state of the traffic ahead, help our cars cope in poor weather conditions and even charge our electric vehicle batteries. In the future, the very roads themselves will help us drive better.

Our reading today includes one of Jesus' most famous statements about himself. He's talking to his disciples just before his death, and in response to their bewildered sense of lostness he says, 'I am the Road.' Perhaps we're used to thinking about that statement in relation to people's salvation – Jesus being the way to the Father – but how might this verse be helpful to us in our decision-making? Yesterday we reflected on the joy of God being our companion; today we reflect on the comfort of knowing that Jesus is the road itself.

This Jesus Road is no hard, indifferent stretch of Tarmac. Jesus is the road that leads us through life's varied landscapes, helping us travel safely no matter the weather conditions. Jesus is the road that carries us into the future, sustaining and strengthening us as we go. At the beginning of John 14, Jesus describes himself as going on ahead of the disciples to a better place (v. 1). Jesus is the road which will bring us to the very best future we could ever imagine.

We will have plenty of decisions to make in life, but let's rejoice that we're travelling on a road which is helping us to drive better.

Take a moment to picture that scene: your life is a car and you're driving it along a road called Jesus. What might that road look like, and how does it feel to be travelling on it?

LYNDALL BYWATER

TUESDAY 22 JULY
JOHN 14:15–27

The helper

'But the Helper (Comforter, Advocate, Intercessor – Counsellor, Strengthener, Standby), the Holy Spirit, whom the Father will send in My name [in My place, to represent Me and act on My behalf], He will teach you all things. And He will help you remember everything that I have told you.' (v. 26, AMP)

Let me extol the virtues of travel agents for a few moments. After years of booking my own holidays – trawling the web for the best deals on flights and hotels, booking my own airport transfers and scouring local tourist information sites for the best way to get from A to B – I booked my most recent holiday with a travel agent. It was bliss! A lovely woman called Donna found me the best deals on everything. She answered all my questions without complaining, and she'll be at the end of the phone if we encounter any problems while we're away. That's what I call a helper.

In our series on good decision-making, we've reflected on God as our companion on the journey, and we've thought about Jesus as the very road we're travelling on. Today we ponder the third person of the Trinity, the Holy Spirit. In today's passage, Jesus is speaking to his disciples shortly before his death. He knows that tough times lie ahead for his beloved friends. He knows that they will have many difficult decisions to make. Yet he doesn't promise them a step-by-step guide; he promises them his own Spirit. He doesn't leave them with a self-help manual; he sends them a helper.

I love the Amplified Version's rendering of verse 26 (see above), as it captures something of the richness of the help the Holy Spirit gives us: the spirit advises us, strengthens us, reassures us, advocates for us and even prays for us. This Spirit sounds even more amazing than the most competent of travel agents! When life's journey brings you face to face with moments of decision, remember that you are not without help. The Spirit of Jesus is in you, bringing you all the wisdom, understanding and strength you need.

Reflect on each of the words used to describe the Holy Spirit in the Amplified Version of John 14:26 (quoted above). If you enjoy writing, you might like to write a short piece in response to each of the words.

LYNDALL BYWATER

WEDNESDAY 23 JULY   **PROVERBS 2**

Wisdom ways

Then you will understand what is right, just, and fair, and you will find the right way to go. For wisdom will enter your heart, and knowledge will fill you with joy. Wise choices will watch over you. Understanding will keep you safe. (vv. 9–11, NLT)

Have you ever learnt a sport and become good at it? If you have, you'll know just how many hours it takes to develop a good technique, and you'll know that, when those crunch moments come – the penalty kick or the match-point serve – it's your technique that enables you to deliver the perfect shot. Beginner's luck can get you so far, but it's skill and consistency that bring in the trophies.

If you were to open the book of Proverbs and search for verses to do with making good decisions, you'd find very little. If you searched for the word 'wisdom', on the other hand, the results go on for pages. That may be because good decisions are like those moments in a game when we suddenly have a crucial shot to make, whereas wisdom is the technique we need to develop in order to make that shot count when the moment arrives.

Today's passage describes something of what it means to grow in wisdom. It talks about tuning our hearts to hear God; storing up treasures of knowledge and understanding; getting to know God; walking paths we know to be good. It's a beautiful picture of a God-centred life. When we choose to live with that kind of integrity, we cooperate with the work of God's Spirit within us to develop what you might call 'wisdom instincts'. Then, when the moment of decision arrives, it's those wisdom instincts which help us know what we should choose.

It would be lovely to think we could just download those wisdom instincts when we need them, install all those wonderful qualities of integrity at the click of a button, but you won't be surprised to hear that it doesn't work like that. Wisdom is cultivated, not downloaded, and it takes time to grow.

Give thanks today for someone in your life who has those 'wisdom instincts'. How have you seen wisdom at work in their life? What might you learn from them, and how can you apply that learning in your own life?

LYNDALL BYWATER

THURSDAY 24 JULY 1 CHRONICLES 28:1–10

Know what's underneath

'And you, my son Solomon, acknowledge the God of your father, and serve him with wholehearted devotion and with a willing mind, for the Lord searches every heart and understands every desire and every thought.' (v. 9, NIV)

Received wisdom suggests that no parent should ever say 'yes' to their offspring's request for a pet until said offspring have asked at least 50 times. Sure, the endless pleading and repetitive refusals might get a bit wearing, but in the end, you'll be glad you stuck it out, because the child who has asked 50 times is far more likely to help walk the dog than the child who only had to ask once or twice. (Though, let's face it, you'll probably end up doing the walking eventually!)

David had an important decision to make. Should he build a temple to the God he worshipped? On the face of it, it was what we sometimes call a 'no-brainer': he had the authority to do it, he had the wealth to do it and he had the desire to do it. Perhaps the most remarkable aspect of this story then is the fact that he didn't do it.

The words in verse 9 are directed to Solomon, but they give us a helpful glimpse into David's decision-making process. God had shown him deep truths about himself. He had come to understand that his warrior nature meant there were passions and motives at work deep in his heart which made him the wrong person for the job of temple-building (v. 3).

We talked yesterday about 'wisdom instincts'. When we make decisions from that place of deep wisdom, we allow God to show us the truth about our motives. We may think we want something, but are we really right for it, and it for us? We may have the ability to do something, but does it fit wth what's going on deep inside us? The great news is that even if we don't know the answers to those questions, God does.

Loving God, you formed my being and you know me completely. Help me to see myself the way you see me – your compassionate gaze shining the light of truth and grace on all that lies hidden deep within me. Amen.

LYNDALL BYWATER

FRIDAY 25 JULY   **PSALM 25:1–12**

Three questions

Show me the right path, O Lord; point out the road for me to follow. Lead me by your truth and teach me, for you are the God who saves me. All day long I put my hope in you. (vv. 4–5, NLT)

When I was a child, I was a big fan of the 'Mr Men' books by Roger Hargreaves. I loved the colourful characters with their equally colourful traits, but what I loved most was that everything was so simple. There were good choices and bad choices, problems and solutions. Mr Happy cheered up Mr Sad, Mr Noisy learnt to talk quietly and Mr Bounce got special weighted boots from the doctor to help him stay grounded (even if he did end up going through the bedroom floor).

If only life were that simple, especially when it comes to decision-making. The easiest decisions are the ones that involve choosing between a bad option and a good option, but most aren't like that. We're usually having to choose between several things which are all good in their own way, or as the psalmist puts it, we're having to find the right path for us in that moment, because we can't travel down all the roads at once.

St Ignatius wrote much on the subject of making good decisions, and he offered three simple questions to help us discern which path God might be pointing us towards.

- The first could be summed up as: 'For me?' This road might be good for many people, but is it the right one for me?
- The second question could be summed up as: 'For now?' This road looks good, and it may even be right for me, but is it right for now, or should I wait?
- The third question could be summed up as: 'For good?' This road may seem to fit for me at this time, but does it feel like it will bear good fruit and draw me closer to God?

If you're praying through a decision, take some time to reflect on it in the light of St Ignatius' three questions. You may not get the final answer straightaway, but listen for the wisdom that comes as you ponder.

LYNDALL BYWATER

SATURDAY 26 JULY — **NEHEMIAH 2:1–18**

Thinking things through

After dark I went out through the Valley Gate, past the Jackal's Well, and over to the Dung Gate to inspect the broken walls and burned gates. (v. 13, NLT)

Connie had been in the study for over an hour. Armed with a cup of tea, Gerry knocked on the door. At her jaunty greeting, he pushed it open to find his wife surrounded by a sea of lists, charts and Post-it notes. 'What on earth are you doing?' he asked. 'Oh,' she said, 'I'm just trying to work out whether we should paint the front door forest green or moss green.'

The way we like to make decisions depends on our personality. Some of us feel most comfortable being intuitive and heart-led, while others love to analyse and calculate. Nehemiah may well have been in the latter group. He wanted to rebuild the walls and gates of Jerusalem, and though his heart had led him to take the project on, his approach was essentially mind-led. He was methodical and analytical, doing a comprehensive survey and making detailed plans. With several miles of wall to build, there must have been hundreds of important decisions to make, but the sense we get is that Nehemiah thought each one through thoroughly.

It doesn't matter whether your decision-making is more heart-led or more mind-led. Both are equally valid. In fact, the most important decisions in life require us to be able to do both. It may help to acknowledge which of the two we find most challenging, because then we can work on it. Are you someone who feels most at ease in your feelings, using your intuition to sense the way forward? If so, why not practise analysing your decisions by making a 'pros and cons' list. Are you someone who likes to see the data and make a well-thought-out choice? If so, why not spend some time looking at art or listening to music, noticing the feelings that stir in you.

Sometimes we need to hear a different voice. Do you have a friend who makes decisions in a different way to you? Why not sit down with them over coffee and get their wisdom on the decision you're making?

LYNDALL BYWATER

SUNDAY 27 JULY   2 KINGS 4:8–37

Feeling it through

She sent a message to her husband: 'Send one of the servants and a donkey so that I can hurry to the man of God and come right back.' 'Why go today?' he asked. 'It is neither a new moon festival nor a Sabbath.' But she said, 'It will be all right.' (vv. 22–23, NLT)

Gerry gazed in bewilderment at the piles of paper on Connie's desk. 'All this, just to work out what shade of green to paint our front door?' 'Of course! I've thought it through carefully and the most logical choice is moss green.' Gerry's wistful silence drew a frustrated sigh from his wife. 'What on earth is the matter?' 'Nothing,' he said, a little nervously. 'It's just that green makes me feel rather glum. Can't we choose a shade of blue instead?'

Yesterday we talked about thinking our way through decisions. Today we're exploring what it means to feel our way through a decision. Like Gerry, some of us prefer to listen to our reactions and our instincts, rather than doing methodical calculations.

Today's story tells of a mother who found herself in a devastating situation. Her son had died in her arms and she must have been beside herself. Yet somewhere beneath the grief was a strong instinct for what to do next. She didn't explain her plan to anyone, even her husband, maybe because she thought he'd think her mad, but deep down, she knew that this was the right thing to do for her boy.

You may have encountered a view that deciding things with the mind is more reliable – facts are better than feelings, etc. – but that's largely a cultural preference. The west has tended to over-value facts and reason, while devaluing instinct and intuition. In other cultures (including the Hebrew culture Jesus was born into), how you feel about something is considered just as valid a way of discerning the right choice as what your logical mind tells you. Our feelings are an intrinsic part of who we are, and they're a gift from God which can steer us just as reliably as our minds can.

Practise listening to your feelings. Each one is like a different voice, and some are louder than others, but each deserves attention. Is there longing? Fear? Hope? Weariness? Joy? Can you capture each feeling in a sentence or two?

LYNDALL BYWATER

MONDAY 28 JULY **PHILIPPIANS 4:4–9**

Praying things through

Don't worry about anything; instead, pray about everything. Tell God what you need, and thank him for all he has done. Then you will experience God's peace, which exceeds anything we can understand. His peace will guard your hearts and minds as you live in Christ Jesus. (vv. 6–7, NLT)

I find myself writing these daily Bible reflections on making good decisions at a time in my life when I have some important decisions of my own to make. God's timing really is spot on! To use the language of the last couple of days reflections, I tend to be a mind-led person when I'm grappling with difficult decisions, and a few weeks ago I found myself going round and round in circles, trying to think about the future, about the choices I have before me, about the pros and cons, about the things stopping me from making the decisions… desperately trying to make it all add up. And then, into the maelstrom, God whispered the word 'prayer'.

From the comfort of my 21st-century life, I can hardly imagine what it was like to be a Christian in Philippi in the first century, but I am confident it wasn't easy. There would have been tough choices to make – sometimes life-and-death decisions – and I imagine life must have often felt uncertain, even chaotic. The Philippians seem to have needed a healthy dose of joy and peace. Paul's response to them was not to counsel them on good decision-making techniques; his response was to remind them to take everything to God in prayer.

Whether we're heart-led or mind-led, we all need to be prayer-led people. There comes a time for all of us when we need to stop trying to find the answer and simply lay the dilemma in God's hands. In fact, we don't just bring our decisions to God, we bring ourselves, with all our anxieties and uncertainties. In prayer, we rest our whole selves in the healing embrace of Christ, and that beautiful, unfathomable peace wraps around us. When we're ready to step back into the world, we find ourselves renewed.

Love of Christ, enfold me. Power of Christ, sustain me. Light of Christ, illumine the path ahead of me. Joy of Christ, kindle afresh in me. Peace of Christ, shield my heart and mind as I hide myself in you. Amen.

LYNDALL BYWATER

TUESDAY 29 JULY PSALM 119:1–16

The truth of God's word

I will study your commandments and reflect on your ways. (v. 15, NLT)

I once heard the story of a remote tribal community who only had a couple of pages of the Bible in their native language. The pages in question were from the book of Jeremiah, which admittedly wouldn't be my choice as a starting point for reading the Bible on account of how gloomy it can be, but when a missionary visited them, he found that they had understood many deep things about God's character from that tiny fragment.

The Bible is a priceless treasure. It comes to us from ancient times, even the most recent parts were written almost 2,000 years ago, yet it contains truth which is as fresh and relevant today as it was when it was first written. The reason that remote tribe could thrive in their Christian lives with just a few pages from the prophet Jeremiah is because every page of the Bible is divinely designed to show us God. The stories may seem alien – Bronze-age cultures and their nomadic wanderings, first-century fishermen and tax-collectors – but the God they encountered is the God we encounter. Through their journeys, we see God's ways; in their stories, we discover God's character.

Looking in the Bible for answers to our dilemmas can be a mixed experience. Given that the net you're dealing with is probably the internet rather than a fishing net, and you can travel further in an hour than most of the people in the Bible travelled in their lifetime, it's safe to say you probably won't find a verse that perfectly reflects your situation. But the verses you do read will help you to see more clearly the God who loves you and who holds all things together, and the more you see of God, the easier it will be to make good choices.

Each time you read the Bible, why not take some time to jot down a few thoughts in answer to the question: 'What do I learn about God's ways and God's character from these verses?'

LYNDALL BYWATER

WEDNESDAY 30 JULY   **PSALM 119:101–112**

The light of God's word

Your words are a flashlight to light the path ahead of me and keep me from stumbling… Your laws are my joyous treasure forever' (vv. 105, 111, TLB)

I attended a boarding school for blind children throughout my childhood, and when I was about ten years old, we began to read various portions of the Bible in Braille. We liked nothing better than playing 'Bible Bingo' after lights-out – opening our Bibles, picking a verse at random and proclaiming it over someone else in the group. We were neither the first nor the last to treat the Bible like some kind of horoscope, but perhaps we did it because, deep down, we wanted those random pronouncements to magically solve our problems.

What does it mean then to turn to the Bible when we've got decisions to make? Psalm 119:105 talks about God's word being a lamp. I like the Living Bible translation's use of the word 'flashlight', because it reminds us that the lamp the psalmist talked about wouldn't have been like the high-powered streetlamps of today. It would've been an oil lamp, held by the traveller, casting a small pool of light which would allow her to see her own feet and the stretch of ground in front of her. It would be enough to show her things which might trip her up, and it would help her see the direction of the road for the next few steps. She would need to keep it close, letting its flame shed light on each new stretch of road and step by step it would help her find her way.

The Bible can't give the solution to every dilemma we face, nor can it show us a high-definition view of our future, but if we keep it close and open it often, it can shed light on where we stand, it can help us avoid pitfalls and it can give us confidence to take our next step.

Are you looking for an answer to your decision-making dilemma every time you read the Bible? Ask the Spirit to help you lay down those unresolved questions so you can receive the word God wants to give you for today.

LYNDALL BYWATER

THURSDAY 31 JULY   **EXODUS 18:8–27**

Hearing the hard words

'If you follow this advice, and if God commands you to do so, then you will be able to endure the pressures, and all these people will go home in peace.' (v. 23, NLT)

In recent years, we've heard an alarmingly large number of stories of abuse at the hands of Christian leaders. (And if you're one of those who has suffered in that way, please know that thousands of us have prayed for you, even if we didn't know your particular story.) The question I find myself asking every time I hear one of these stories is: did anyone ever confront that leader about the decisions they were making? Sadly, it seems voices of challenge and disagreement are all too rare around those who have a lot of power.

Like so many leaders before and since, Moses had got to a place where he was unable to see that his decisions were unwise, so God sent him what you might call a 'critical friend'. Our studies over the past two weeks have focused a lot on how we make good decisions for ourselves, but at some point we will need to bring others into our decision-making. That's just part of being human, and that moment had arrived for Moses.

Jethro was Moses' father-in-law, and he was clearly someone Moses trusted. All sorts of people might want to share their opinions about the decisions we're making, but the best ones to listen to are the ones who know us and love us and whom we trust. Jethro didn't mince his words. He was honest and clear, which might have been a bit painful for Moses, but it helped him see a different perspective. Then, having voiced his opinion, Jethro refocused Moses on God's will and God's commands.

The council of others is important in decision-making because it helps us see ourselves and our motives more clearly, but the wisest advisers will always encourage us to go back to God before we make the final decision.

Looking back, who are the people who have been helpful to you in your decision-making? In what ways did they help you? Are you aware of times when you've helped others make decisions? In what ways did you help them?
LYNDALL BYWATER

FRIDAY 1 AUGUST ACTS 1:12–26

The divine decider

So they nominated two men… Then they all prayed, 'O Lord, you know every heart. Show us which of these men you have chosen as an apostle to replace Judas in this ministry… ' Then they cast lots, and Matthias was selected to become an apostle with the other eleven.
(vv. 23–26, NLT)

AI has revolutionised my takeaway-buying experience. Instead of agonising over the many options available, my fellow diners and I simply give each option a number (being careful to eliminate any we know we wouldn't want), then ask the nearest smart speaker to pick a number for us at random. It's gloriously adventurous and it's never failed us yet.

We've mined various Bible treasures about making good decisions, but the one we haven't examined yet is the use of lot-casting. Perhaps it makes you feel a bit uncomfortable. I mean, it's one thing to use dice-throwing or coin-tossing for choosing something trivial like a takeaway, but is that really a godly thing to bring into a decision-making process?

In our modern western culture, when someone suggests tossing a coin, they are usually choosing to allow chance to be the final decider, but that's not how ancient Hebrew culture understood lots. Lots were a way to know God's will in a decision. It's also important to note that even lot-casting was a cooperation between the community and God. They didn't cast lots in a vacuum. The disciples began by discerning together which two candidates to choose between. Then they prayed, and only then did they cast the lot. When it fell to Matthias, they were certain he was God's choice.

We tend not to use lots in our decision-making now, but we can still be alert to things which seem random, circumstances we have no control over which somehow speak into our decisions. Notice the unexpected things which catch your attention: the odd coincidences, the words that keep cropping up, the signs which seem to keep pointing you in one particular direction. Ponder them; talk about them; pray about them. There's every chance they're God speaking to you.

Buy or make a promise box: a box full of slips of paper, each containing a promise from the Bible. Then pick one out each time you pray. Enjoy the way God brings you surprising encouragement through your random selection.

LYNDALL BYWATER

SATURDAY 2 AUGUST   **MATTHEW 6:19–34**

Trust

'For the pagans run after all these things, and your heavenly Father knows that you need them. But seek first his kingdom and his righteousness, and all these things will be given to you as well.' (vv. 32–33, NIV)

One of the greatest skills of parenting is the ability to give your children the freedom to make choices about their own life, while also making sure that they get what they need. It's a fine balance, and it's easy to veer towards being overly controlling or overly permissive. I don't have children of my own, but I give thanks for parents who kept me safe and enabled me to thrive, while also helping me develop the independence to follow my own path.

This beautiful art of parenting is the palest reflection of what our loving creator God has been doing ever since the dawn of time. The fact that we can spend two weeks reflecting on how to make good decisions is testimony to the fact that we have the freedom to make decisions at all. We began these reflections in the garden of Eden (Genesis 1—3), where God blessed Adam and Eve with self-determination, giving them freedom to take possession of their earthly home. The God who brought us into being has designed us to grow to maturity.

Yet that same parent heart cannot abandon us wholly to our own devices. As Jesus told his disciples, our needs are known to our Father in heaven – our physical needs for food, clothing and shelter, and our emotional needs for love, significance and purpose. No matter how self-determining we become, this divine parent still longs to protect us and provide for us.

We started this series of notes rejoicing in the truth that God walks with us, and we end the series giving thanks that God cares for us. We can never be sure where our decisions will take us in the end, but we can put all our trust in the one who's looking after us.

Trusting God is a great idea, but how do you need to practise it today? Do you need to practise faith instead of worry? Do you need to stop trying to solve something? Do you need to ask for help?

LYNDALL BYWATER

Amos: prophet for a disappointed God

Amy Boucher Pye writes…

Hello! We're back for our second week of studying the message of Amos, the prophet called to deliver God's judgement on his people who have moved away from him in their embrace of wealth, prosperity and a strong army. This book can feel like a tough read, but I promise we'll find gems of encouragement along the way.

When I think about Amos, what strikes me is his obedience in following God's call and leaving everything that was familiar to him – his fig trees and sheep in what was probably a ruggedly beautiful setting – to deliver his unpopular message to the northern kingdom. He willingly travelled to Israel, those who had left the united kingdom behind as they pursued their own prosperity and their own gods (yes, those two golden calves). They rejected him and his message, but Amos remained true to the living God.

Although Amos' message can feel hard and discouraging at times, behind it is a God who cares so deeply that he's willing to deliver these words of judgement. After all, if he had lost his love for them, he would have just turned away completely. The fact that he uprooted Amos and sent him as an uncultured foreigner to speak hard words reveals God's love and commitment to his people. It makes me think of the saying, uttered by Holocaust survivor Elie Wiesel and others, 'The opposite of love is not hate; it's indifference.' We see from the strongly worded judgements and proclamations that God is anything but indifferent.

In this latter half of Amos, we'll encounter him in a funeral setting crying out loudly with deep emotion as he laments how God's people have turned away from God. He also shares several disturbing visions that include God's meting out of the consequences for their wayward hearts. The book, however, ends on a high note with promises of the new wine that will flow down the mountains when God restores Israel, rebuilding their cities once again.

I pray you will be strengthened through these days with Amos, knowing that God cares for you deeply.

SUNDAY 3 AUGUST — AMOS 5:1–17

A way to lament

Hear this word, Israel, this lament I take up concerning you: 'Fallen is Virgin Israel, never to rise again, deserted in her own land, with no one to lift her up.' (vv. 1–2, NIV)

We can imagine Amos delivering his lament for the fall of Israel, God's beloved nation, while donning sackcloth and expressing his emotion loudly. Even as he uttered the words about God causing 'wailing in all the vineyards' (v. 17), so he may have sobbed with the pain of this message. Their great sins and many offences – their lack of interest in the things of God – have caused God to let them experience the consequences of their actions. Here Amos grieves this sad situation.

These verses employ a literary structure of repetition around some opposing themes (for this insight I'm grateful to Gary V. Smith in the *NIV Application Commentary*). We start with (a) the lament of the death of the nation (vv. 1–3), followed by (b) Amos' call to seek God and live (vv. 4–6), followed by (c) the accusations of no justice (v. 7). At the centre (d) is the resounding hymn to Yahweh, the one who created the star constellations and who 'turns midnight into dawn' (vv. 8–9). Moving back through these themes, we return to (c) the accusations of no justice (vv. 10–13), followed by (b) Amos' call to seek God and live (vv. 14–15), before returning to (a) the lament of the death of the nation (vv. 16–17).

Why does this format matter? Often the writers of the Old Testament use literary devices to help them voice their laments. Having a system to use helps to release the ideas and thoughts. Recently, for instance, I recommended to a grieving friend to write an acrostic lament – a poem starting successively with the letters of the alphabet. It's a way to express what might feel too hard to otherwise voice to God.

Help me, Lord, to hate evil and love good. I know you promise to be with me and that you are who you say you are. Amen.

AMY BOUCHER PYE

MONDAY 4 AUGUST   AMOS 5:18–27

True worship

'Away with the noise of your songs! I will not listen to the music of your harps. But let justice roll on like a river, righteousness like a never-failing stream!' (vv. 23–24, NIV)

Those in Israel longed for the 'day of the Lord' – the time of reckoning when God would enjoy a final victory over his enemies. However, Amos questions why they would yearn for this when it would expose the evil deeds of their hearts. (Interestingly, the first use of this term 'day of the Lord' in the Bible is here in Amos.)

Notice again how Amos' vivid language, employing that with which he was familiar, makes for riveting reading. Someone flees a lion but meets a bear; he arrives to the safety of his home but rests his hand on a snake (v. 19). As we read, we feel a sense of relief followed by doom and despair.

After Amos grabs their attention, he delivers God's verdict – God only wants true worship, neither the assemblies that are a 'stench' to him (v. 21) nor their music, which sounds like noise (v. 23). God knows they aren't following him wholeheartedly; instead they have 'lifted up the shine of [their] king' (v. 26). God won't tolerate idol worship; he demands all of their devotion and praise.

Notice that in the midst of these hard-to-read statements there is one glorious verse that bolsters our hope: 'But let justice roll on like a river, righteousness like a never-failing stream!' (v. 24). The image of running, living water is one we find throughout the Bible, including when Jesus names himself as the source of living water: 'Whoever believes in me, as Scripture has said, rivers of living water will flow from within them' (John 7:38).

As we return to God, he will fill us with his living water. We need not follow the ways of Israel here, especially as we've been given the gift of the indwelling Holy Spirit.

Jesus, stream of living water flowing from within me, refresh me and renew me, that I might sparkle for you. Amen.

AMY BOUCHER PYE

TUESDAY 5 AUGUST AMOS 6:1–14

A sobering oath

The Sovereign Lord has sworn by himself – the Lord God Almighty declares: 'I abhor the pride of Jacob and detest his fortresses; I will deliver up the city and everything in it.' (v. 8, NIV)

Amos appears to be speaking at a funeral banquet, but the wealthy people to whom he aims his message seem less than interested. Instead of looking out for the poor and needy, sharing with them even the lesser cuts of meat, they 'dine on choice lambs and fattened calves' (v. 4) and 'drink wine by the bowlful' (v. 6). Instead of working for the betterment of society, they 'lie on beds adorned with ivory and lounge on [their] couches' (v. 4).

God's chosen and beloved people are not supposed to be so inward-focused, so selfish and proud. God will not abide by this behaviour; we read a chilling oath against them: 'I will deliver up the city and everything in it' (v. 8). Oaths at that time carried weight and respect, and an oath from God, whose character was faithfulness, would involve a covenant that could not be broken.

We might recoil at the thought of God's judgement, but notice the vivid language Amos employs on behalf of God as to why he reaches this point: 'You have turned justice into poison and the fruit of righteousness into bitterness' (v. 12). The people have been feeding others poison when they should have been extending the meat of justice; they were serving up rancid flesh instead of the fruit of righteousness.

I invite you to ponder God's judgement in a sinful world. How do you feel knowing that those who do wrong will ultimately be held to account? When you think of systemic evil, or the wrongs hidden by culture, consider if God is calling you to be his agent of truth and grace. Know that God hasn't given up on the world and the people he has created.

'For the word of the Lord is right and true; he is faithful in all he does. The Lord loves righteousness and justice; the earth is full of his unfailing love' (Psalm 33:4–5).

AMY BOUCHER PYE

WEDNESDAY 6 AUGUST   **AMOS 7**

Idols in high places

This is what the Sovereign Lord showed me: the Sovereign Lord was calling for judgement by fire; it dried up the great deep and devoured the land. Then I cried out, 'Sovereign Lord, I beg you, stop! How can Jacob survive? He is so small!' (vv. 4–5, NIV)

We come to a series of chilling visions that Amos shares with God's people, those who have moved from him in practice and devotion. Having had enough of their hardened hearts, God outlines the consequences of their actions.

Notice in the early part of this passage how many times God is called 'sovereign' – Amos acknowledges that, unlike the rest of God's people, he knows that the Lord is the true and living God and there is no other. He also makes the case to this mighty and all-powerful creator that Jacob is 'so small'; how can he survive? (vv. 2, 5). Amos' heartfelt pleas brim with emotion, and we see God relent. But God will not be moved on destroying the disgusting idolatry that has filled the high places of Israel, the sanctuaries (v. 9). God will brook no rivals.

Amaziah, an apostate priest, doesn't want to hear Amos' declarations and seeks to have him exiled back home to Judah. Amos threatens his power base, and so he seeks to retaliate. Note how this priest voices his allegiance not to God but to the king: 'Don't prophesy any more at Bethel, because this is the king's sanctuary and the temple of the kingdom' (v. 13). Amos defends his calling – it's not something he sought, after all – and leaves the priest with a disturbing pronouncement of the judgement he will suffer as acted out on his family (v. 17).

As you read and ponder this story, I invite you to ask God if there are places in your heart that are increasingly given over to the idols of our day – relationships, work, influence and so on. If you discern any, ask God to help you to dismantle them as you worship him fully, with joy.

Jesus said: 'But the Advocate, the Holy Spirit, whom the Father will send in my name, will teach you all things and will remind you of everything I have said to you' (John 14:26).

AMY BOUCHER PYE

THURSDAY 7 AUGUST   **AMOS 8**

Empty ritual

The Lord has sworn by himself, the Pride of Jacob: 'I will never forget anything they have done. Will not the land tremble for this, and all who live in it mourn?' (vv. 7–8, NIV)

I'm guessing that most of us, at some point during a church service, have let our thoughts drift to the week to come, our to-do lists or our projects. Through Amos, God speaks sternly to his people who take this wandering state of mind further – they who can't wait for the sabbath to be over, 'that [they] may market wheat' (v. 5) and continue swindling the poor. God shows himself to be fiercely protective of the vulnerable and downtrodden and will not let his people continue in their showy religious performances. He can see into their hearts and knows that what they care about most is wealth and influence – not him or others.

Because God is all powerful, he can and will reveal these empty rituals for what they are: 'I will turn your religious festivals into mourning and all your singing into weeping' (v. 10). The famine will be not only of food but more critically of God's word, as the people, now bereft, 'stagger from sea to sea' as they search for it (v. 12).

As we read through the sins of this wealthy class of God's people, we might distance ourselves from them. Sure, we might think, sometimes my mind wanders during the sermon, but surely God won't judge me too harshly, right? It is true that he offers us forgiveness when we return to him, running towards us with open arms of love, and I don't want to discount that amazing gift. But I'm pondering how we can attune our hearts so closely to him that we are connected to him throughout the moments of our days. As we surrender to him, he will connect us, through the Holy Spirit, to his very self.

Loving Father, welcoming Jesus, comforting Spirit, help me to welcome you into all areas of my life. I want to practise your presence and enjoy your love. Amen.

AMY BOUCHER PYE

FRIDAY 8 AUGUST AMOS 9:1–10

Special no more

'Are not you Israelites the same to me as the Cushites?' declares the Lord. 'Did I not bring Israel up from Egypt, the Philistines from Caphtor and the Arameans from Kir? Surely the eyes of the Sovereign Lord are on the sinful kingdom.' (vv. 7–8, NIV)

Amos' final vision is damning. God's people have not repented; they have not destroyed the idols in their places of worship and returned to him with an undivided heart of devotion. God therefore has no choice but to destroy this temple – Bible commentators believe it's the one at Bethel with the golden calf and not the main one in Jerusalem. For them, the sanctuary is not a place of refuge; they assumed they could hide behind their empty rituals and that God would protect them, but there is no escape (vv. 2–3).

Why is God so concerned? Verse 7 helps us here, as God asks them if they are any different to their neighbours. They can reply only in the negative. He brought them to the promised land to be a people set apart for him, those chosen to receive his love and to serve him with a pure heart, but they have proved to be no different than the other peoples – the Cushites, Philistines and Arameans. The original listeners may have wondered why the prophet mentioned the Cushites, as this people were far away in Africa. The next two people groups were their sworn enemies, which emphasised how far they had gone in their rejection of God. They were not living out their covenantal relationship and had now dropped to the same level as the people previously driven out from the land.

Perhaps a response to this stark reading for those of us who believe in God and enjoy an intimate relationship with him is to pray earnestly for those who do not know him. As you ponder, who comes to mind? God is gracious and forgiving, and we can be his hands and feet to share his saving love with others.

Loving God, help me to be fully committed to you; I don't want to waver in my belief. Help me too to share your loving message of hope and acceptance. Amen.

AMY BOUCHER PYE

SATURDAY 9 AUGUST   **AMOS 9:11–15**

New wine

'I will bring my people Israel back from exile. They will rebuild the ruined cities and live in them. They will plant vineyards and drink their wine; they will make gardens and eat their fruit. I will plant Israel in their own land, never again to be uprooted.' (vv. 14–15, NIV)

Friends, we've made it! Well done for persevering through this challenging book of prophecy. I know that it's felt hard to confront the ways God's people disappointed him again and again, and to hear his displeasure and pronouncements of judgement. But his sadness comes from his great love for them.

Amos pivots in these last verses to give some welcome words of hope. Some theologians wonder if Amos wrote these or if they were added by a later editor. They feel different in tone than the earlier decrees, but he was probably speaking to a much smaller remnant.

Amos speaks of a time when the Israelites will once again enjoy God's blessings, when God will repair the broken walls and restores the ruins (v. 11), meaning that the nation will be re-established. In doing so, God will bring his people back from exile to live in a fertile land of abundance. The extent of this lush growth will be such that those sowing the new crops (in that climate, in October or November) will be hindered by the continued harvesting of the previous crops (which normally would finish in August or September).

What glorious promises of lavish crops and a complete restoration of the nation. Although we know that God was speaking to his people through Amos, and the original context stands, we too can find hope trusting the wonders that await us when he enacts his new kingdom. As we read in Revelation: 'And I heard a loud voice from the throne saying, "Look! God's dwelling-place is now among the people, and he will dwell with them. They will be his people, and God himself will be with them and be their God"' (Revelation 21:3). May it be so, now and always!

Almighty God, thank you that you love your people so much, even when we hurt you. Help me to put into practice all that I've gained from this Old Testament prophecy. Amen.

AMY BOUCHER PYE

Confidence in God

Catherine Butcher writes:

How can we build confidence in who God is and what he has done for us? Over the next two weeks we will be looking at different Bible characters who put their confidence in God. Then we will consider what God has done for us, building confidence in Jesus, his death, resurrection and the promise of eternal life with him.

We start with Abraham, whose confidence in God was tested to the limit when he thought it meant sacrificing his only son.

Joseph began life as an overconfident young man, but learned through tough situations that God works for our good even when life seems bad.

Like many of us, Moses lacked self-confidence, but found support from his brother Aaron and his friend Hur. Like them, we need not face life's difficulties alone.

Caleb's confidence in God didn't waiver, even though it was 45 more years before he saw the land God had promised him. Hannah also had to wait for God's promise to be fulfilled. She struggled with infertility, but eventually God gave her a much longed-for child. Even before she fell pregnant, she put her confidence in God and worshipped him.

Mary, a virgin, was confident that God could be trusted, even though the promise of a son was humanly impossible. Simeon and Anna had been waiting confidently for God to send the promised Messiah. They held on to the promises God had made and trusted that he would keep his promises.

Like each of these characters, we need to learn to trust God – but our prayers aren't always answered in the ways we expect. Rachel Gardner's story and each of the contemporary stories you will read over the next fortnight, show that the God of history is the same today. Sometimes he's a God of surprises, but he can always be trusted.

How can we be confident? We have scripture and the new covenant Jesus has given us. We can be confident in Jesus' resurrection and, like Peter and the martyrs, we can be confident that death is not the end.

The apostle Paul based his confidence on the reality of the resurrection and the transformation God's Holy Spirit brings to lives; confidence that looks forward to Jesus' second coming and our eternal home in heaven.

I hope you will take encouragement from these short stories and studies as God builds your confidence in his never-failing love for you.

SUNDAY 10 AUGUST **GENESIS 22:1–18**

Abraham trusts God's promise

'The fire and wood are here,' Isaac said, 'but where is the lamb for the burnt offering?' Abraham answered, 'God himself will provide the lamb for the burnt offering, my son.' (vv. 7–8, NIV)

As a teenager, I felt called to learn how to write about Jesus in jargon-free language that unchurched people would understand, but I failed English A-level. My slip-sliding faith journey finally came to a stable place when I began to put my confidence in God for myself, rather than as an inheritance from godly parents. After training as a journalist, I launched a county-wide free magazine, but the project failed after five issues. A prophetic word that God would use my writing to affect the nation seemed like a delusion. Fortunately, God is capable of taking failure and making his masterpieces. Many years later, when the Commonwealth celebrated the late Queen's 90th birthday, more than 1.3 million copies of a book about her faith were distributed by churches. I had the privilege of writing it with author Mark Greene. It was unique as the Queen had written the foreword.

Like Abraham I had to learn to put my confidence in God and not my own abilities. When Abraham was first told that God would make him into a great nation, it seemed like a pipedream. When he was getting old, and was still childless, he questioned God, who reminded him: 'a son who is your own flesh and blood will be your heir' (Genesis 15:4). Determined to fulfil the promise through his own efforts, he fathered a child with his wife's servant Hagar. Finally, he and Sarah had a son of their own. Abraham learned to put his confidence in God. While it does raise some difficult moral questions, even when God seemed to want him to sacrifice the boy, Abraham obeyed and trusted.

Where does your confidence lie? Are you trusting God's promises? Is your identity rooted in him? Do you rely on him to provide for all your needs?

Heavenly Father, thank you for loving me and for adopting me as your child. Help me to put my confidence in you as the source of my identity, my provision and my hope for the future. Amen.

CATHERINE BUTCHER

MONDAY 11 AUGUST **GENESIS 50:1–21**

Joseph's misplaced confidence

'You intended to harm me, but God intended it for good to accomplish what is now being done, the saving of many lives'. (v. 20, NIV)

The night before her execution in 1915, Edith Cavell told the chaplain who brought her Communion, 'Standing as I do in view of God and eternity, I realise that patriotism is not enough; I must have no hatred or bitterness towards anyone.' Together they sang the hymn 'Abide with me', praying:

Hold thou thy cross before my closing eyes.
Shine through the gloom and point me to the skies.
Heaven's morning breaks and earth's vain shadows flee;
in life, in death, O Lord, abide with me.

Edith put her confidence in God and the certainty of heaven. She became the most prominent British female casualty of World War I, and her death was credited as a reason that the United States entered the war in April 1917. As a result, the war ended more quickly, and many lives were saved.

Joseph, in today's reading, was an overconfident young man, favoured by his father and hated by his ten older brothers. His life story could be seen as a series of disasters: rejected by his siblings; sold into slavery; wrongly punished. But his confidence in God shone through as he responded to every adversity with faith. When his brothers finally realised who he was and came to him in fear, he forgave them, just as Edith Cavell forgave her betrayers and her executioners. Joseph saw that his brothers' wicked plans had turned out for good and, from his high position in Egypt, his strategy had saved people from famine.

What obstacles are you facing today? Financial difficulties? Health problems? Relationship breakdown? Maybe life hasn't turned out as you expected. How are you responding to life's difficulties? Ask a friend to pray through these issues with you, asking God to give you confidence that he is working for your good.

The psalmist asks three times: 'Why, my soul, are you downcast? Why so disturbed within me?' The response is this challenge: 'Put your hope in God' (Psalm 42:5). How can you do that today?

CATHERINE BUTCHER

TUESDAY 12 AUGUST   **EXODUS 17**

Moses' helpful friends

When Moses' hands grew tired, they took a stone and put it under him and he sat on it. Aaron and Hur held his hands up – one on one side, one on the other – so that his hands remained steady till sunset.
(v. 12, NIV)

When the Revd Canon Alyson Lamb was diagnosed with stage four gall bladder cancer in January 2023, she was offered chemotherapy but declined it. 'I chose quality over quantity of life,' she wrote to me later that year. 'Looking back over the past ten months, I'm very glad I did! Because of this illness God has presented me with new opportunities to do what I love best: to speak with others about Jesus; to share the life and hope he promises; and to pray with those who wish it… neighbours, hospital staff, tradespeople, first responders, chance encounters. Such a joy and privilege… I feel that the months since diagnosis have been the sweetest and most carefree of my life.'

At her funeral a close friend talked about how she and Alyson had met to pray together every week. Others described their deep friendships, as well as Alyson's confidence in Jesus. Her confidence in God and those friendships sustained her to the end.

Moses had led a privileged life in Pharaoh's palace, but he fled into the desert after murdering an Egyptian who was mistreating a Hebrew slave (Exodus 2:11–15). His fiery encounter with God in the desert (Exodus 3:1—4:17) showed him he could be confident in God, but he was unsure of himself and asked God to send someone else (4:13). Moses returned to Egypt, supported by his brother Aaron and holding the staff which God had used to show his power. He chose to be mistreated with the people of God (Hebrews 11:24–25), then led them out of slavery. Even though he experienced many signs of God's power at work through him, he needed Aaron and Hur to support him when he was weak.

Paul told the Thessalonians to 'encourage one another and build each other up' (1 Thessalonians 5:11). Think about your fellow Christians and church leaders. How can you encourage them this week?

CATHERINE BUTCHER

Caleb: opportunities not obstacles

'My fellow Israelites who went up with me made the hearts of the people sink. I, however, followed the Lord my God wholeheartedly.' (v. 8, NIV)

Matt Parfitt, the founder of Grace Enterprises (GE), gave up his career as a teacher to become an ethical employer, putting his faith into practice. His vision is to see lives transformed through working in a supportive environ-ment in the sustainable enterprises that GE has set up, like gardening, cleaning, marquee hire and biscuit-making. The GE workers are people with major obstacles to employment, such as drug addiction and alcoholism. In GE's first seven years, more than 100 people overcame those obstacles and were helped into employment through the different GE businesses, which continue to expand.

Caleb was a similar man of faith. He had been one of the spies sent out to explore the promised land (Numbers 13). They all saw the obstacles to taking possession of the land, but Caleb's confidence was in God. As a result, he was one of only two adults who set out from Egypt to reach the land God had promised them. His confidence didn't waiver, even though it was 45 more years before they finally entered the land. When they did, Caleb asked for the 'hill country' (v. 12) – the difficult terrain – as his inheritance. He was 85 years old but was able to say: 'I am still as strong today as the day Moses sent me out' (v. 11).

At the start of our journey of faith we can feel confident, only to become half-hearted when life isn't a bed of roses. Sometimes we need to go back to basics to remember what God has done for us in Christ. I find that telling others about Jesus, or helping on an Alpha course is a wonderful reminder of why I'm following Jesus. Let's be like Caleb, confident in God's promises and serving him wholeheartedly to the end of our lives.

Paul said, 'My only aim is to finish the race and complete the task the Lord Jesus has given me – the task of testifying to the good news of God's grace' (Acts 20:24). Ask for God's help to do this.

CATHERINE BUTCHER

THURSDAY 14 AUGUST   **1 SAMUEL 1**

Hannah's change of heart

Eli answered, 'Go in peace, and may the God of Israel grant you what you have asked of him.' She said, 'May your servant find favour in your eyes.' Then she went her way and ate something, and her face was no longer downcast. (vv. 17–18, NIV)

Rachel Gardner, Girls Brigade president and director of partnerships at Youthscape, posted on Facebook one Mothering Sunday about her struggles with motherhood:

> *All the years I fought to be a mum, I experienced my body as a collection of broken and dying places; silent womb, empty breasts, vacant lap. I listened in sorrow-tinged wonder to the tiny fluttering hearts of little ones hidden deep in other women's bodies. I was in awe. I was in pain… One day I said no to further treatment… and I said a tentative yes to adoption. Yes, to having my heart woven into stories that had already begun. Yes, to heartbeats already fluttering in other wombs, other places.*

Rachel and her husband now have two adopted children: 'We began as strangers with nothing to tie us together, except a deep hope that love will weave us into each other, forever.'

Hannah's story ended differently as she gave birth to Samuel. For years Hannah had gone to the temple with her husband and his other wife, who had children and provoked her till she wept. The priest, Eli, saw her 'great anguish and grief,' and he prayed that God would grant her request.

We will never know why some prayers go unanswered. Many women, like Rachel, struggle to conceive. Somehow Hannah knew that God was going to answer her prayer. Her expression changed. She worshipped God and went home to make love to her husband.

Like Hannah, many of us have prayed for years about issues that seem unchanged. God's ways are often different from ours, but he does promise to work for good in the lives of those who love him (Romans 8:28).

'God is our refuge and strength, an ever-present help in trouble. Therefore we will not fear, though the earth give way' (Psalm 46:1–2). Let's trust God, even when we don't understand what he is doing.

CATHERINE BUTCHER

FRIDAY 15 AUGUST   **LUKE 1:26–56**

Mary's confidence in God's word

'For no word from God will ever fail.' 'I am the Lord's servant,' Mary answered. 'May your word to me be fulfilled.' (vv. 37–38, NIV)

After 21 years bringing up our children in the same house, we were moving. However, just as all the furniture had been loaded into the removal van, our buyer put a stop on the sale. For complicated reasons we had to exchange and complete on the same day; she had every right, and we had no redress. We spent the evening in our empty house reliving happy memories, but wondering if we would be back the next day unpacking and starting the hunt for a buyer again.

That night I dreamed that the new house was ours and that God's word to us was: 'Open up, ancient gates… let the King of glory enter' (Psalm 24:7, NLT). 'The glory of this present house will be greater than the glory of the former house… And in this place I will grant peace' (Haggai 2:9).

Our new house had six-foot-high gates that had always been shut when we visited. The next day, miraculously and exceptionally, our estate agent solved the problems with our buyer. We headed to the new house and flung the gates wide open. Hundreds of people have visited since then and many comment on how peaceful it is.

God's word to Mary was beyond her wildest imagination, but she was confident that God could be trusted. God's word to her was confirmed by scripture ('The virgin will conceive and give birth to a son' – Isaiah 7:14), by her cousin Elizabeth, and by the fact that it came true – tests that give us confidence in God's word to us.

Like Mary, we might be troubled or afraid at a turn of events. But, when we love him, we can be confident that God can work for good in difficult situations even when we don't understand what's happening.

'We know that in all things God works for the good of those who love him, who have been called according to his purpose' (Romans 8:28). Are you confident that this is true? Ask God to help you trust him.

CATHERINE BUTCHER

SATURDAY 16 AUGUST   LUKE 2:22–40

Simeon and Anna

There was also a prophet, Anna… She was very old; she had lived with her husband seven years after her marriage, and then was a widow until she was eighty-four. She never left the temple but worshipped night and day, fasting and praying. (vv. 36–37, NIV)

For decades, Kath's home in Eastbourne was a centre known for warm hospitality, regular Bible teaching, individual counselling and prayer, craft evenings, music and much more. Kath had been a missionary. When she married, she and her husband set up the ministry in Eastbourne. Like Anna, Kath was widowed after a few years, but she continued to welcome guests from around the world, as well as closer to home, until ill health and increasing years meant the house had to be handed over to a different charity. Kath's confidence in Jesus was infectious, and her ministry encouraged all those who visited her to put their confidence in Jesus for themselves.

Simeon and Anna were confident that the promised Messiah would come. Simeon's confidence was based on a revelation by the Holy Spirit that he would not die before he had seen the Messiah with his own eyes (v. 26). Anna was committed to a life of worship, fasting and prayer (v. 37), and she recognised Jesus as the promised Messiah when Mary and Joseph brought him to the temple to fulfil the requirements of the law.

Both Simeon and Anna were advanced in years, but they had not given up hope. Anna's situation as a widow in a patriarchal society would have been much more difficult than it is today. She thrived by keeping her focus on God.

In Hebrews we read: 'Therefore, since we are surrounded by such a great cloud of witnesses, let us throw off everything that hinders and the sin that so easily entangles. And let us run with perseverance the race marked out for us, fixing our eyes on Jesus, the pioneer and perfecter of faith' (12:1–2).

Let's follow the examples of Simeon, Anna and people like Kath – trusting God, whatever our circumstances.

Pray today for the older Christians you know, asking God to show you how to encourage their faith. Ask God to fill you afresh each day with his Holy Spirit, enabling you to persevere in faith to the end.

CATHERINE BUTCHER

SUNDAY 17 AUGUST   **LUKE 1:1–25**

Confidence in scripture

I myself have carefully investigated everything from the beginning, I too decided to write an orderly account for you, most excellent Theophilus, so that you may know the certainty of the things you have been taught. (vv. 3–4, NIV)

As a journalist I was often sent to report on court proceedings. Sometimes I believed both the prosecution and the defence witnesses, but more seasoned legal experts could spot the lies, especially when witnesses' stories were too similar. I stressed that fact at a meal arranged for my fellow journalists where our guest speaker highlighted the differences in the four gospels. Matthew wrote for Jews and emphasised Jesus as the coming king, so he included the story of wise men at Jesus' birth. Mark's focus was on Jesus as a servant; there is no birth account. (Who records a mere servant's birth details?) Luke was writing for a Gentile audience and highlighted Jesus' humanity, noting the shepherds' worship in Bethlehem. John focused on Jesus' divinity; his first chapter takes us back to creation and the amazing fact that the creator of the universe made his home with us on earth.

Because these gospel accounts are different, we can have more confidence in their truth than if they had all been identical. Luke wanted us to be certain about Jesus' life, death and resurrection. As a doctor, he included many stories of Jesus healing people. Also, he often mentioned women, like Elizabeth, as those whom Jesus honoured.

Experts in textual criticism, who aren't necessarily Christians, recognise that the gospels accurately represent what the authors of these books originally wrote.

The fact that Jesus was a historical person is backed up by the Roman historian and senator Tacitus writing around AD116 and the Jewish historian Josephus, writing around AD93–94.

As you read Luke's gospel and other scriptures, you can have confidence that they are an accurate record of Jesus' life. Ask the same Holy Spirit who filled John the Baptist to guide you into all the truth (John 16:13).

'All Scripture is inspired by God and is useful to teach us what is true and to make us realize what is wrong in our lives' (2 Timothy 3:16, NLT). Invite God to speak to you through scripture today.

CATHERINE BUTCHER

MONDAY 18 AUGUST   **EXODUS 12:1–30**

Confidence in a new covenant

When the Lord goes through the land to strike down the Egyptians, he will see the blood on the top and sides of the door-frame and will pass over that doorway, and he will not permit the destroyer to enter your houses and strike you down. (v. 23, NIV).

When I look at the unleavened Matzo bread, used by Jewish people at Passover, I'm amazed to see that it is pierced. And, in the Passover celebration, three Matzo are used – but only one is broken and hidden. Through the centuries, Jewish people have followed God's instructions to celebrate this family feast, remembering how God set them free from slavery in Egypt. The symbols they use remind them of the first Passover, but also have significance for Christians remembering Jesus, part of our triune God.

When Jesus celebrated Passover with his disciples for the last time (Luke 22:7–20), he gave new significance to the bread and the wine. They all knew about the old covenant made between the Hebrew people and God. Now Jesus was declaring a new covenant with his blood: no longer the blood of sacrificed animals.

Today, as we celebrate Holy Communion/the Breaking of Bread/the Eucharist, or whatever your church calls this feast, we remember Jesus' death and celebrate his resurrection, with the new understanding that his death was a once-for-all sacrifice. His body was broken to make us whole; his blood was spilt on the cross to cover over our sins so that God sees us as justified by Jesus – that's just as if I'd never sinned!

The apostle Paul explained: 'Whenever you eat this bread and drink this cup, you proclaim the Lord's death until he comes' (1 Corinthians 11:26). We proclaim the victory of his crucifixion to principalities and powers. As we celebrate and put our confidence in the death and resurrection of Jesus, we also look forward to his second coming, when we will drink wine with Jesus at his wedding feast (Matthew 26:29).

When you next celebrate Communion, ask God to give you a new confidence in Jesus' resurrection victory.

'Can anything ever separate us from Christ's love? Does it mean he no longer loves us if we have trouble…' (Romans 8:35, NLT). Proclaim Jesus' victory over your life and have confidence in his love, whatever you are facing.

CATHERINE BUTCHER

TUESDAY 19 AUGUST   **1 CORINTHIANS 15:1–28**

Confidence in Jesus' resurrection

For what I received I passed on to you as of first importance: that Christ died for our sins according to the Scriptures, that he was buried, that he was raised on the third day according to the Scriptures.
(vv. 3–4, NIV)

After a series of strokes, Vic had to spend his remaining years in a nursing home. His wife visited daily, but Vic wanted to go home – home to be with Jesus. He was confident that Jesus has gone before us: crucified – yes; dead and buried – yes; but now resurrected and interceding for us (Romans 8:34) as he prepares a place for us to be with him forever (John 14:1–4). Vic was confident in the resurrection.

All four gospels describe Jesus' crucifixion. Historians have little doubt that he died. Suggestions that he swooned and the cool of the tomb revived him beggar belief. Crucifixion was the cruellest of deaths and to ensure that he was dead, a spear was thrust through his side (John 19:34). The blood and water which then flowed was medical proof that he was dead.

The tomb was guarded by Roman soldiers so no one could remove the body. If the body had been stolen by the Jews, it would have been reproduced to disprove rumours of resurrection. If the disciples had taken Jesus' dead body, would they have been prepared to go to their deaths believing in his resurrection and declaring he was God?

After his resurrection Jesus appeared to hundreds of people, and the accounts of his post-resurrection appearances to Mary, the twelve disciples, the followers on the Emmaus Road, Paul and 500 others (vv. 5–6) were recorded within the lifetime of witnesses. The disciples were transformed from frightened cowards to bold witnesses proclaiming their unshakeable belief that Jesus was alive.

As Paul put it, belief in the resurrection is 'of first importance' (v. 3). Because Jesus rose from the dead, we can have confidence that death is not the end for us either: 'Death has been swallowed up in victory' (v. 54).

Jesus is 'the firstborn from among the dead' – now with his Father 'making peace through his blood, shed on the cross' (Colossians 1:18–20). Thank God for Jesus, who makes it possible for us to have life after death.

CATHERINE BUTCHER

WEDNESDAY 20 AUGUST   **ACTS 5:17–42**

Peter and the martyrs

'God exalted him to his own right hand as Prince and Saviour that he might bring Israel to repentance and forgive their sins. We are witnesses of these things, and so is the Holy Spirit, whom God has given to those who obey him.' (vv. 31–32, NIV)

Modern martyrs are not unlike the early disciples who rejoiced because they had been counted worthy of suffering for Jesus' sake (v. 41). The threat of imprisonment or death does not diminish their confidence in God or stop them proclaiming the good news that Jesus is the Messiah (v. 42).

I was privileged to work with Baroness Caroline Cox, researching her book *The Cox's Book of Modern Saints and Martyrs*. One modern martyr was Mehdi Dibaj, who was killed in 1994. He told an Iranian court: 'I am not only satisfied to be in prison for the honour of his Holy Name, but am ready to give my life for the sake of Jesus my Lord and enter his kingdom sooner.'

In more recent times many Iranians have found refuge in the UK; some have even started Farsi-speaking churches. One Iranian man I have spoken to left his wife, job and country because the leader of the church he had started to attend in Iran had been imprisoned. He feared he would be next.

Peter and the other disciples were persecuted for talking about Jesus but remained confident in God. In today's reading, an angel was sent to bring them out of prison. They could have taken their captivity as a warning to stop preaching. Instead, they headed for the temple courts to teach more.

Peter continued to preach and was persecuted for it. The third-century Christian scholar, ascetic and theologian Origen of Alexandria, wrote that Peter was eventually martyred by being crucified hea-downwards in Rome.

Modern martyrs and these early martyrs all put their confidence in God, who gave them the strength to face their accusers. Today, thank God for their witness and pray that you will also have the confidence to speak about Jesus.

Visit the websites of charities that support the persecuted church throughout the world, and see how you can be praying for your brothers and sisters. Use Psalm 71 as a prayer for them and for others you know who face hardship.

CATHERINE BUTCHER

THURSDAY 21 AUGUST ACTS 17:16–34

Paul's confidence in Jesus

'As I walked around and looked carefully at your objects of worship, I even found an altar with this inscription: to an unknown god. So you are ignorant of the very thing you worship – and this is what I am going to proclaim to you.' (v. 23, NIV)

Celebrity tattoo artist Kat Von D told Allie Beth Stuckey on her 'Relatable' podcast that she started looking into new age spirituality when she was in her 20s: 'I was searching for answers and meaning in so many of the wrong places.'

Although she ran a successful tattoo business in LA, Kat admits she was an alcoholic. She said: 'I was very lucky that I had parents who were Christians. In my darkest moments, intuitively I was praying.'

Her journey to faith began in 2019, when Kat's husband's questions prompted her to rethink a lot of issues, including her spirituality. She told Allie Beth that she had thrown away books on witchcraft, the occult, yoga and meditation and said, 'I don't want those crutches in my life anymore. I just want Jesus… they don't align with who I am and who I want to be.'

When she was baptised, some people accused her of staging a publicity stunt, but she says, 'I'm on fire for Jesus and I don't plan on this dying out. The more I learn, the more excited I am.'

Paul saw the spiritual hunger in Athens. Rather than dismissing the outward appearance of their idol-worshipping culture, he was confident that they were searching for spiritual truth. He looked for ways to connect with them, quoting their poets; Jesus' resurrection was the basis for his confidence.

Think about the people you meet. Maybe they are covered in tattoos like Kat Von D. Perhaps they are enthusiastic about new age practices. Maybe they seem very different from you. But might they be on a journey, searching for spiritual truth? How could you pray for them and help them to discover the sure foundation for spirituality that can only be found in Jesus?

Father, forgive me when I dismiss people who don't seem to be like me. Help me to find ways to identify and connect with people who are open to hearing more about Jesus. Give me grace and courage to speak. Amen.

CATHERINE BUTCHER

FRIDAY 22 AUGUST   **EPHESIANS 4**

Confident in transformation

Get rid of all bitterness, rage and anger, brawling and slander, along with every form of malice. Be kind and compassionate to one another, forgiving each other, just as in Christ God forgave you. (vv. 31–32, NIV)

The foreword to a book of prisoners' stories I compiled* reads: 'These 40 stories are a vital reminder of the hope that Jesus gives. They show how lives can be transformed, and forgiveness can be found in the most unlikely places. There is no one, no life, no story that is beyond God's power to love and transform into renewal.'

In the book, the Revd Paul Cowley MBE, founder of Caring for Prison Leavers, tells how God transformed his life from one of 'drink, divorce, debt and despair'. What changed? He explains: 'I did an Alpha course. God just completely hit me between the eyes and said, "I love you. I want to rescue you. I want to help restore you, and I want to reintegrate you into a normal healthy family."'

Paul Cowley and the apostle Paul both experienced the same transforming power that changes each of us, making us acceptable to God.

As the apostle Paul wrote to the Ephesians about the life that we should live as those transformed by God's love, he was aware how much his own life had been transformed. He had been a fierce opponent of Jesus' disciples. He watched as Stephen was stoned to death after preaching a powerful sermon that outlined God's rescue plan for the Jewish people, showing how they had resisted the Holy Spirit's work (Acts 7:51, 58).

Once Jesus changed his life, the apostle Paul went on to be a powerful preacher, the author of much of the New Testament and, most of all, a man who was confident that he was forgiven for his past and empowered by God's Holy Spirit to live a new life, pleasing to God.

---

*40 Stories of Hope: How faith has changed prisoners' lives (CWR, 2017)

Which areas of your life need more of God's transforming work? Paul writes about our heart attitudes, our thought-life, our actions and our speech. Invite God's Holy Spirit to continue his transforming work in your life.

CATHERINE BUTCHER

SATURDAY 23 AUGUST   **REVELATION 21**

Confidence in heaven

'"He will wipe every tear from their eyes. There will be no more death" or mourning or crying or pain, for the old order of things has passed away.' (v. 4, NIV)

Peter Pickett was in his 90s when he recorded a video for his great grandchildren. He wanted them – and all of us who attended his funeral – to know 'whatever the situation is, there is always hope in Jesus'. The hymns and readings he had chosen for the event pointed to the hope of heaven. The Bible reading – Revelation 21 – described the heavenly home he was looking forward to.

Journalist, author and satirist Malcolm Muggeridge once said: 'The only ultimate disaster that can befall us… is to feel ourselves to be at home here in earth. As long as we are aliens, we cannot forget our true homeland.'

Heaven is that homeland. In his most intimate conversation with his disciples, just before he was crucified, Jesus talked about his Father's house and said, 'I am going there to prepare a place for you' (John 14:2).

The heavenly home we read about in today's reading is John's apocalyptic vision of a place without pain or tears. It is a new beginning for the earth and for our relationship with God. John struggled to describe it. He used the images of precious stones, and words like brilliance and glory. Most significantly, he knew that there would be no more death. Instead, there will be continuous refreshment from 'the spring of the water of life' (v. 6).

A recent Theos study, *Ashes to Ashes: Beliefs, trends, and practices in dying, death, and the afterlife*, quoted a YouGov poll in 2021 which found that only 33% of UK adults believe in an afterlife; 42% do not. Christians can be confident that there is life beyond this one as Jesus has promised. It is good news that is worth sharing and, like Peter Pickett, it is something to be shared with everyone we know.

The psalmist wrote: 'Even when I am old and grey, do not forsake me, my God, till I declare your power to the next generation' (Psalm 71:18). Ask God for opportunities to pass on your faith to the next generation.

CATHERINE BUTCHER

Paul's letter to the Philippians

Sara Batts-Neale writes…

I remember clearly the childhood moment when I first grasped what an epistle was: real letters, from real people to real communities. I love letter writing myself – even now, something arriving in the post is worth far more than the price of a stamp. A letter means someone cared enough to take extra effort to be in touch, rather than only sending a text or instant message. Letters are real tokens of love across time and distance. That is exactly what Paul's letter to the Philippians represents. The community of Christians in the Roman colony of Philippi are his joy, and he longs to be reunited with them.

I wonder what it would it be like if people kept my notes of encouragement or condolence and used them as the basis for teaching in the future. Fortunately, I suspect that's not likely to happen. But happily for us, the careful first-century preservation and copying of letters means we too can reflect on the challenging, instructive and pastoral words sent to some of the first followers of Jesus Christ.

Paul writes to the Philippians from prison, although no one's quite agreed on where he was imprisoned at the time. Many think it was Rome, dating the letter to around AD61–63. His first visit to Philippi was ten years earlier. If you have time, take a few minutes to read Acts 16, where you can find the backstory to this letter. In Philippi Paul met and baptised Lydia and her household, from whose home the church began. He also fell into trouble, being flogged and imprisoned. That led to the baptism of Paul's jailor and his household – after, that is, a miraculous loosening of prison chains.

It's helpful to be able to put this subsequent letter into context, but it also makes us wish that the letters from the Philippians were also preserved – what was in the two-way correspondence? Wouldn't it be wonderful to be able to eavesdrop on the whole conversation rather than just Paul's side? What we do know is that he had deep pastoral concern for the community he founded. We know that they, in turn, had supported him financially. We also find Paul's words – of encouragement, love, generosity, perseverance, humility, partnership and on the nature of Christ – which inform our lives of faith today.

SUNDAY 24 AUGUST **PHILIPPIANS 1:1–11**

Past, present and future in partnership

I thank my God for every remembrance of you, always in every one of my prayers for all of you, praying with joy for your partnership in the gospel from the first day until now. (vv. 3–5, NRSV)

In the opening sentences, Paul remembers with thanks, prays for current circumstances and looks forward to the future. That's a rather good model for our Christian life – gratitude for what has been; attention to the here and now; prayers for the places, people and work to which we are called.

Paul writes 'to all the saints in Christ Jesus who are in Philippi' (v. 1) – a salutation that gives them an enduring theological and geographical identity. In other words, they are in relationship to God, and in relationship to place. We are, too. Our identity is shaped by our life in Christ, but also by the places we inhabit.

We too are called to be us in our time and our place. We too are part of God's work of sharing the gospel. I love the idea that we, who live thousands of years and miles apart, are linked to that community by a common thread of purpose. We too are in partnership with Paul, sharing in God's grace. The one who was at work in the Philippian community is at work in us today. Paul's prayer for the Philippians can become our prayer, too – that the love we experience in Christ will help us grow and learn, so that we may determine how best to live.

We, the unique and precious children of God, are loved for who we are now. We can give thanks for what has been – for the past versions of ourselves we have left behind; places we have lived; people we have loved and been loved by. We are a product of all that has gone before – the sum of all our decisions – including deciding to follow Christ as Lord. Our future and our identity are found in our discipleship.

We're shaped by place, whether we've been rooted to the same spot or are practically nomadic. Offer thanks to God for the place you live now, and the ways it has formed your life and faith.

SARA BATTS-NEALE

MONDAY 25 AUGUST PHILIPPIANS 1:12–30

Encouragement in all circumstances

I want you to know, brothers and sisters, that what has happened to me has actually resulted in the progress of the gospel. (v. 12, NRSV)

Our honeymoon destination was Cuba, but storms delayed outward travel, stranding us in Madrid overnight. Granted, that's not quite the inconvenience of jail or shipwreck like Paul experienced! Despite frustrating events, we stayed cheerful and dealt surprisingly well with the setbacks.

Paul looks on the bright side of his imprisonment, encouraging his beloved Philippians who are also living in troubled times. Paul is using his presence with the imperial guard for good. By now, he's told everyone about Jesus! I wonder if the original jailor from Acts 16 was listening to this news snippet. I can imagine the jailor nodding along in recognition of Paul's character.

Today's passage encourages us to live the gospel in whatever circumstances we find ourselves. Paul initially shares dismay that some people were proclaiming Christ for their own self-interest, but he concludes that actually, that is not important. He just rejoices that the good news is being shared. We too can be encouraged. *How* we share is far less important than the fact we *are* sharing it – so let us be bold in whatever we do.

Boldness is one of the words I think some of us might have internalised as negative. Like assertiveness being decried as bossiness, boldness is a trait we women can be criticised for. Our boldness about our faith is rooted in conviction that we do indeed know the God of truth, and trust in Christ as Lord. Let us take the encouragement from Paul's prison experience to be bold in our speaking of the word!

'O give thanks to the Lord; call on his name; make known his deeds among the peoples' (Psalm 105:1).

SARA BATTS-NEALE

TUESDAY 26 AUGUST | **PHILIPPIANS 2:1–18**

Humility and stardom

For it is God who is at work in you, enabling you both to will and to work for his good pleasure. (v. 13, NRSV)

I wonder if all Christians since Paul's letter was first read have felt that they were living through a 'crooked generation'! We're no different as we survey rapid changes around us. It's less than 20 years since smartphones arrived, altering how we communicate, bank and shop – and shaping the lives of young people. Reality TV tempts with instant stardom. Not quite the starriness Paul meant when he described the Philippians as shining like stars!

The right kind of starriness arises when we acknowledge God's work within us, seeing our need for humility. Looking to others' interests rather than our own is countercultural in a society that places the individual first and encourages us to prioritise our needs above those of others. 'Being of the same mind' is a very difficult thing to do in any community, but Paul wanted the Philippians to strive for unity. His instructions help them do just that – to live with compassion and sympathy.

Regarding others as better than ourselves isn't a call to think worse of ourselves by the way. The humility that recognises our need for God and leads us to stop being selfish or conceited doesn't require us to take a path of self-abasement.

The poem or hymn to Christ in verses 6–11 could have either been already in circulation or Paul's original work – we're not sure. What we do know is that it's probably the oldest statement of faith we have. It's still authorised for use in our churches today. It tells us not just of Christ's humility, his willingness to walk alongside as servant, but also of his exalted status. A slave, but one whose very name should be revered. A hymn that encourages us to remember the might and majesty of Jesus, in whom we find our unity.

'Let your light shine before others, so that they may see your good works and give glory to your Father in heaven' (Matthew 5:16).

SARA BATTS-NEALE

WEDNESDAY 27 AUGUST   **PHILIPPIANS 2:19–30**

Paul's coworkers in the faith

I am the more eager to send him, therefore, in order that you may rejoice at seeing him again and that I may be less anxious. (v. 28, NRSV)

One of life's hardest things is to wait for news of a loved one's illness. Even waiting for good news can have us on edge. Messages can seem to take forever, and we jump every time the phone pings. It's easy to have sympathy with the Philippians who were so worried about Epaphroditus. Epaphroditus was probably the envoy who had delivered the Philippians' gift to Paul, so they would have known and loved him. No wonder they were distressed when they found out he was ill and would have been rejoicing to have him restored to health and returned to them. It is a great reminder for us that whatever our work for Christ, we work in community with other Christians.

The relationships Paul describes between himself and Timothy – 'as a son with his father' – and Epaphroditus – 'brother, co-worker and fellow soldier' (vv. 22, 25, NIV) – speak to deep bonds of love and trust in their work and life together. Timothy's concern for others is loud and clear on the page. I wish we knew more about him and Paul's other co-workers.

My experience as a chaplain has shows me time and time again that the value I can add is in genuine pastoral concern. Sure, it helps in the occasional conversations to be able to offer a theological insight or a biblical reflection, but mostly, the key to building relationships has been in genuinely caring about the other – seeking to understand, to pray for, and to connect with staff and students who very often have no prior knowledge of the Christian church.

I recognise that the work I do is done as part of the wider community of faith – it isn't down to me alone. Paul's letters show us that he was a concerned pastor to his congregations, but we know he didn't work alone. Who do we work with that we can give thanks for today?

Is there someone known to you today who is unwell? Pray for them now. Offer thanks to God for the healthcare and communications we have available to us today.

SARA BATTS-NEALE

THURSDAY 28 AUGUST   **PHILIPPIANS 3:1–11**

Defining ourselves in Christ

Yet whatever gains I had, these I have come to regard as loss because of Christ. (v. 7, NRSV)

In today's passage, we see a shift from concerns about individuals to teaching about false teachers and pride. I find myself wondering what the Philippians struggled with again and again. I know very well that I am liable to mess up in predictable ways – I suspect the same was true for them!

When Paul writes of flesh and spirit, it is easy for us to focus on specific sins – gluttony, sexual sin – the sorts of things that the word 'flesh' seems to conjure up for me, at any rate. While these are definitely some of the problem, they are not the whole story. One way of thinking about Paul's warning is to think about the difference between paying attention only to our own selfish desires or being oriented towards God. It's less a list of specific sins, and more about better or worse predispositions in life.

We also reflect on Paul's inheritance in the flesh – his unassailable ancestry. Paul is critically aware of his own former privileges – he reels his credentials off, one after the other. But these things now count for nothing. His deep faith replaces all his legally perfect behaviour. That doesn't matter now. Paul can lose all things – money, status, freedom – and see only the value of his knowledge of Jesus Christ. Paul longs for the Philippians to see in him the model for their lives.

What would the lists look like for us if we defined ourselves as Paul did – our inheritances, job titles, accomplishments? Which of those would we happily relinquish, and which are harder to surrender? Just as the Philippians needed reminders that there were pitfalls ahead, so we need reminders that our worth is in our worship of Jesus Christ, not in our job title, marital status or bank balance.

'I became a servant of this gospel by the gift of God's grace given me through the working of his power' (Ephesians 3:7, NIV).

SARA BATTS-NEALE

FRIDAY 29 AUGUST   **PHILIPPIANS 3:12–17**

Perseverance and pressing on

Forgetting what lies behind and straining forward to what lies ahead, I press on towards the goal, towards the prize of the heavenly call of God in Christ Jesus. (vv. 13–14, NRSV)

I've run lots of races and I've never won once – in fact, I have been very nearly last in a half-marathon. Luckily times have never mattered as much as the experience, especially in an event like the Great North Run. Being part of a big race is such a rich metaphor for life – all participants, with different backgrounds and reasons for being there, all making progress towards the same finishing line. Some are sprinting, some barely lifting their feet, but all of them pressing on. I think that's such a lovely phrase. Press on. Just keep moving. It speaks to me of perseverance, of the value in small steps alongside giant strides – and of keeping the end in mind.

An organised race will have signposts and marshalls, making it hard to get lost, but running or walking an unfamiliar trail by ourselves is a different matter. Without a good map, we run the risk of losing our way – the more so if we stop paying attention to the landscape around us. In the same way, if we don't keep our lives focused on Christ, it is perilously easy to become sidetracked. Paul talks of those whose god is their belly and whose minds are set on earthly things; a focus on self, possessions, accomplishments is a distraction from the path of life in Christ. That's the wrong kind of orientation we reflected on yesterday.

Paul encourages the Philippians, and therefore us too, to not worry about what is past: status, our mistakes, disappointments and blunders. We carry on – some days taking small steps – in the knowledge that Jesus walks with us.

'Therefore, since we are surrounded by so great a cloud of witnesses, let us also lay aside every weight and the sin that clings so closely, and let us run with perseverance the race that is set before us' (Hebrews 12:1).

SARA BATTS-NEALE

SATURDAY 30 AUGUST **PHILIPPIANS 4:1–9**

Love for the Philippians

Therefore, my brothers and sisters, whom I love and long for, my joy and crown, stand firm in the Lord in this way, my beloved. (v. 1, NRSV)

Throughout the week we have seen how Paul loves the Philippians. Their support of him is reflected in his joy in their community. In these verses, Paul guides them and encourages them as they learn how to lean on the Lord. There is a call for unity and rejoicing. Despite Paul's own admitted anxieties (see 2:28), he reminds them how to find peace. The exhortation 'Do not be anxious about anything' (v. 6) is always easier on paper than in practice.

If you need someone to do worst-case scenario planning, you should call me. I am definitely a worrier. Sometimes, it's a practical help. I've not missed a train in nearly 20 years. (Although, I've also spent quite a lot on tea while waiting around at railway stations!) It's perilously easy to use verse 6 like a formula, dismissing the fears and worries of others as symptoms of a weak faith. I can tell you from experience this is not an encouragement to hear.

Paul wants to encourage habits of thought and prayer that will naturally lead to rejoicing, secure in the knowledge that the Lord is near. Worry can be all-encompassing – but giving our brain a break by focusing on what is good is proven to be beneficial. Verse 8 gives us a good benchmark for whether something is worthy of our energy and attention. Very often our worries and worst-case scenarios aren't true – they're just familiar, and we think they're true. Something somewhere is always worthy of praise; we just need to be looking for it in order to be able to notice it. It's a simple formula: keep on doing what we've learned and seen in Paul and we'll remember daily that God is with us.

What one habit of prayer and praise can you practise today? Perhaps it's something new or different, or maybe something that's slipped from your routine. Commit to it this weekend.

SARA BATTS-NEALE

SUNDAY 31 AUGUST   **PHILIPPIANS 4:10–23**

Generosity, gratitude and kindness

I've found the recipe for being happy whether full or hungry, hands full or hands empty. Whatever I have, wherever I am, I can make it through anything in the One who makes me who I am. (vv. 12–13, MSG)

Money isn't just money. It represents many different things – freedom, purchasing power, authority – and very often, it's a proxy for love. It's the same here. The Philippian church supported Paul through very difficult times. He doesn't quite say 'thank you' today, but we can see they have been looking out for his needs. Paul has been glad of the gift which represents their love. Paul is at pains to say he welcomes the gift not for his own enrichment but because it emphasises the richness of their partnership, which dates back to the beginning of his missionary ministry. It is the Philippians' practical outworking of faith.

Verses 11 and 12 are Paul's reflection on learning to live in changing circumstances. Verse 13 is a recognition that whatever life has thrown at him, he can rely on Christ, the one who strengthens. So far so good. But we often see verse 13 quoted as a call to individual triumph or ambition or, even worse, as justification that we should do all things – creating burdens of responsibility and exhaustion.

Jesus is Lord of everything – our concerns matter to him, and we shouldn't stop discerning his will for us. But sometimes that might involve laying things down rather than setting ourselves impossible targets. And, like Paul, finding happiness and gratitude whatever our circumstances.

Tomorrow is the start of September, which for many heralds the start of a new school year – new targets, new ambitions, new routines. We can take strength to cope with change from the knowledge and love of Jesus. We can remember the idea from last Sunday that we're called to live our life in our places and in Jesus, with gratitude, no matter where we are. As Paul says, 'To our God and Father be glory forever and ever. Amen' (v. 20, NRSV).

'Come to me, all you who are weary and are carrying heavy burdens, and I will give you rest' (Matthew 11:28, NRSV).

SARA BATTS-NEALE

BRF Ministries

Inspiring people of all ages to grow in Christian faith

BRF Ministries is the home of Anna Chaplaincy, Living Faith, Messy Church and Parenting for Faith

As a charity, our work would not be possible without fundraising and gifts in wills.
To find out more and to donate,
visit brf.org.uk/give or call +44 (0)1235 462305

Registered with **FUNDRAISING REGULATOR**

To order

Online: **brfonline.org.uk**
Telephone: **+44 (0)1865 319700**
Mon–Fri 9.30–17.00

Delivery times within the UK are normally 15 working days. Prices are correct at the time of going to press but may change without prior notice.

BRF

Title	Price	Qty	Total
Day by Day with God (May–Aug 2025) – single copy	£5.25		
Day by Day with God (Sep–Dec 2025) – single copy	£5.25		

POSTAGE AND PACKING CHARGES			
Order value	UK	Europe	Rest of world
Under £7.00	£2.00	Available on request	Available on request
£7.00–£29.99	£3.00		
£30.00 and over	FREE		

Total value of books	
Donation	
Postage and packing	
Total for this order	

Please complete in BLOCK CAPITALS

Title .... First name/initials .... Surname ....

Address ....

.... Postcode ....

Acc. No. .... Telephone ....

Email ....

Method of payment

❏ Cheque (made payable to BRF) ❏ MasterCard / Visa

Card no. ☐☐☐☐ ☐☐☐☐ ☐☐☐☐ ☐☐☐☐

Expires end M M Y Y Security code ☐☐☐   Last 3 digits on the reverse of the card

We will use your personal data to process this order. From time to time we may send you information about the work of BRF Ministries. Please contact us if you wish to discuss your mailing preferences. Our privacy possible is available at **brf.org.uk/privacy.**

FR Registered with FUNDRAISING REGULATOR

Please return this form to:
BRF Ministries, 15 The Chambers, Vineyard, Abingdon OX14 3FE | **enquiries@brf.org.uk**

For terms and cancellation information, please visit **brfonline.org.uk/terms**.

Bible Reading Fellowship (BRF) is a charity (233280) and company limited by guarantee (301324), registered in England and Wales

SUBSCRIPTION INFORMATION

Each issue of *Day by Day with God* is available from Christian bookshops everywhere. Copies may also be available through your church book agent or from the person who distributes Bible reading notes in your church.

Alternatively, you may obtain *Day by Day with God* on subscription direct from the publisher. There are two kinds of subscription:

Individual subscription
covering 3 issues for 4 copies or less, payable in advance (including postage & packing).

To order, please complete the details on page 144 and return with the appropriate payment to: BRF Ministries, 15 The Chambers, Vineyard, Abingdon OX14 3FE

You can also use the form on page 144 to order a gift subscription for a friend.

Group subscription
covering 3 issues for 5 copies or more, sent to one UK address (post free).

Please note that the annual billing period for group subscriptions runs from 1 May to 30 April.

To order, please complete the details on page 143 and return with the appropriate payment to: BRF Ministries, 15 The Chambers, Vineyard, Abingdon OX14 3FE

You will receive an invoice with the first issue of notes.

> All our Bible reading notes can be ordered online by visiting
> **brfonline.org.uk/collections/subscriptions**

All subscription enquiries should be directed to:
BRF Ministries, 15 The Chambers, Vineyard, Abingdon OX14 3FE
+44 (0)1865 319700 | **enquiries@brf.org.uk**

DAY BY DAY WITH GOD GROUP SUBSCRIPTION FORM

> To set up a recurring subscription, please go to
> **brfonline.org.uk/day-by-day-with-god**

The group subscription rate for *Day by Day with God* will be £15.75 per person until April 2026.

☐ I would like to take out a group subscription for .... (quantity) copies.

☐ Please start my order with the September 2025 / January 2026 / May 2026* issue. I would like to pay annually/receive an invoice* with each edition of the notes. (*delete as appropriate*)

Please do not send any money with your order. Send your order to BRF Ministries and we will send you an invoice.

Name and address of the person organising the group subscription:

Title .... First name/initials .... Surname ....

Address ....

.... Postcode ....

Telephone .... Email ....

Church ....

Name and address of the person paying the invoice if the invoice needs to be sent directly to them:

Title .... First name/initials .... Surname ....

Address ....

.... Postcode ....

Telephone .... Email ....

We will use your personal data to process this order. From time to time we may send you information about the work of BRF Ministries. Please contact us if you wish to discuss your mailing preferences. Our privacy policy is available at **brf.org.uk/privacy.**

Please return this form to:
BRF Ministries, 15 The Chambers, Vineyard, Abingdon OX14 3FE
enquiries@brf.org.uk

For terms and cancellation information, please visit **brfonline.org.uk/terms**.

Bible Reading Fellowship is a charity (233280) and company limited by guarantee (301324), registered in England and Wales

DAY BY DAY WITH GOD INDIVIDUAL/GIFT SUBSCRIPTION FORM

To order online, please visit **brfonline.org.uk/collections/subscriptions**

☐ I would like to give a gift subscription (please provide both names and addresses)
☐ I would like to take out a subscription myself (complete your name and address details only once)

Title _____ First name/initials _____ Surname _____

Address _____

_____ Postcode _____

Telephone _____ Email _____

Gift subscription name _____

Gift subscription address _____

_____ Postcode _____

Gift subscription (20 words max. or include your own gift card):

_____

_____

Please send *Day by Day with God* beginning with the September 2025 / January 2026 / May 2026 issue (*delete as appropriate*):

(*please tick box*)	UK	Europe	Rest of world
1-year subscription	☐ £21.30	☐ £29.55	☐ £35.25
2-year subscription	☐ £40.20	N/A	N/A

Optional donation to support the work of BRF Ministries £ _____

Total enclosed £ _____ (cheques should be made payable to 'BRF')

Please charge my MasterCard / Visa with £ _____

Card no. ☐☐☐☐ ☐☐☐☐ ☐☐☐☐ ☐☐☐☐

Expires end M M / Y Y Security code ☐☐☐ Last 3 digits on the reverse of the card

We will use your personal data to process this order. From time to time we may send you information about the work of BRF Ministries. Please contact us if you wish to discuss your mailing preferences. Our privacy policy is available at **brf.org.uk/privacy**.

Please return this form to:
BRF Ministries, 15 The Chambers, Vineyard, Abingdon OX14 3FE
enquiries@brf.org.uk

For terms and cancellation information, please visit **brfonline.org.uk/terms**.

Bible Reading Fellowship is a charity (233280) and company limited by guarantee (301324), registered in England and Wales